SCALING
THE WALL

KATHY HICKS

SCALING THE WALL

Overcoming Obstacles to
Missions Involvement

Kathy Hicks

Authentic
LIFESTYLE

Gabriel
Publishing

Waynesboro, Georgia

Published in the USA by Gabriel Publishing
PO Box 1047, 129 Mobilization Dr, Waynesboro, GA 30830
(706) 554-1594 gabriel@omlit.om.org

ISBN: 1-884543-77-4

Published in the UK by Authentic Lifestyle
an Imprint of Authentic Media
PO Box 300, Kingstown Broadway,
Carlisle, Cumbria, CA3 0QS, UK
www.paternoster-publishing.com

ISBN: 1-85078-538-4

Unless otherwise noted, all Scripture taken from the NEW AMERICAN
STANDARD BIBLE ®, Copyright © 1960, 1962, 1963, 1968, 1971, 1972,
1973, 1975, 1977, 1995 by The Lockman Foundation. Used by permission.

Image: ©Corbis
Cover Design: Paul Lewis

Printed in the United States of America

Dedication

To Bonnie Witherall,
   who lived her life showing the love of Jesus to those who needed to hear and gave her life doing the thing Jesus called her to do.
   "Precious in the sight of the LORD is the death of His godly ones." Psalm 116:15

To Gary Witherall,
   who chose to forgive rather than hate, to trust God in spite of his loss, and to present himself as a living sacrifice for the sake of the gospel and the kingdom of God.

   "I urge you therefore, brethren, by the mercies of God, to present your bodies a living and holy sacrifice, acceptable to God, which is your spiritual service of worship." Romans 12:1

Contents

Foreword

It is a great privilege to write a few words about this very unique, cutting-edge, and unusual book. This is a book that grew out of dynamic action at the OM exhibit at Urbana when young people were asked to write on a huge wall what was on their hearts.

I have always felt that it is important to hear what is on a person's heart, as we can learn so much from that. It helps us develop discernment, which is so important for whatever we do with our lives.

It's a long road from making your initial decision for missions to seeing your missions dream become a reality. This book will be a huge help on that road.

I know Kathy Hicks, and she is a person of great experience and wisdom. She also walks the talk. I believe you will be helped and blessed as you take the time to read this very, very special book.

George Verwer
International Director of Special Projects
and Founder of Operation Mobilization

PART ONE:
INTRODUCTION

1

The Wall

As I watched the men on our team take down the Wall I felt something. Sadness? Regret that what it held would be lost? I assumed it would end up in the storage area of OM USA, where the entire display booth would be stored until there was another opportunity to use it.

I didn't care that the rest of the display would be out of sight in storage. After all, it was merely boards, paint, and hardware that created a place for almost sixty members of Operation Mobilization from around the world to interact with and encourage those who came by. Our display was one of 320 representing mission agencies and schools that were at the Urbana 2000 Student Mission Convention to help 19,000 college students find out how and where they could get involved in worldwide missions.

It had been an exciting five days of worship, teaching, interaction, and prayer for these participants. For us it had been a great time to share about the ministry of OM and the opportunities we could offer these students in over eighty countries around the world. But more than that, it had been a time to share a vision of what can be accomplished when people step out in faith, get past whatever obstacles they are facing, and use creative ways to share their faith.

Our booth was constructed to provide some unique opportunities to share that vision. It had a loft from which our media guys controlled the lights, cameras, monitors, and sound for the stage, which every hour produced a different, fifty-minute live program. Sometimes these programs demonstrated swing dancing, juggling, or drama skits, showing how these skills can be used to draw a crowd, begin relationships, and provide opportunities to share one's faith. Sometimes other ministries were highlighted on stage and then prayed for.

While these programs were going on, at the other end of the booth, people were donning costumes and having their pictures taken. They were positioned in front of a green screen. But what the TV monitor and their pictures showed were the students in a country overseas doing evangelism. Some were showing a Bible to a man in front of one of the OM ships. Others were handing a piece of literature to a woman in Central Asia. We wanted them to picture themselves in missions, to see what could be possible if they would step out in faith and obedience.

While all this was happening, the OM representatives were talking with those who had questions. We were there to find out how the Lord was speaking to their hearts, especially at this conference. We wanted to help these college students get the information they needed, even if it meant taking them to another organization's booth whose ministry was more in line with where the Lord was calling them. We prayed with them about their future and the things they were struggling with. And then we encouraged them to write on the Wall.

One side of the Wall was the backdrop for the stage, but behind the stage the Wall was totally white except for these words at the top:

"Let the peoples praise you, O God; let all the peoples praise you. Father, I offer you these things that might limit me from doing my part in seeing the nations worship you . . ."

These words reflected the theme of Urbana that year. We encouraged the students to write on the Wall, to express what was in their hearts—and write they did.

Some wrote prayers of dedication, others confessions. Some were articulate paragraphs; many were lists of words. Most were in English; some were in foreign languages. In all there were almost 700 entries filling the twelve-foot by eight-foot wall.

It didn't seem right that these heartfelt expressions would be hidden away in a storage garage after the conference. Here was insight into the struggles of this new generation of potential missionaries. Shouldn't this information be used somehow? Couldn't it help us find ways to help them get beyond the obstacles they are facing?

I was delighted a few days later to walk into the chapel of OM USA's headquarters and find the Wall reassembled. Others must have felt as I did, that these expressions must be shared, not hidden. It remained there for a couple of months. About once a week our staff would stand around it, praying for those who had poured out their hearts and lifting their concerns to the Lord. It was a real point of interest to those who visited our office, including OM leaders and missionaries traveling through. The comment, "These should be put into a book somehow," was often heard.

My husband Rick, president of OM USA, was invited to speak at a retreat for one of our teams in Europe. While there the conversation turned to what had happened at Urbana and the Wall. Again the thought that this information could be used and should be put into a book was expressed—and that is when it got personal for me. Suddenly I could envision the book—how it could be organized and used to encourage those wanting to join missions to overcome the obstacles they face. Having co-authored books before, I knew I could do this, and suddenly I *wanted* to do it.

Rick called back to the office to make sure they didn't store the Wall away before we got home. He asked that someone begin to record the words that were written and found out that a young man in our office had already begun the process. He too believed that these words should be put into a book and was sitting with his laptop in front of the Wall, copying down the comments (at least all the English ones).

So that's where this book began, with the heartfelt expressions of students at Urbana. But as those of us who are already in missions know, these obstacles are not unique to these students, or even this generation. They are the same ones we have faced and seen the Lord overcome when He called us into missions. The vision of this book is not merely to document the obstacles but also to encourage you by sharing real stories of how God has overcome these same obstacles in the lives of others. We want you to be able to rejoice in seeing that our God is bigger than our fears and circumstances, and that He acts on behalf of those who follow His will.

2

Seeing What God Can Do

There is nothing more inspiring than hearing an exciting, true story about someone overcoming a personal obstacle and obtaining a cherished, yet seemingly unreachable goal. It encourages us to know that these things actually happen to real people, that God reaches down into their lives, arranges circumstances and events, and works in people's hearts to bring about His plan for them. These stories give us hope to believe that if God can do it for them, He just might do something similar for us!

That is why you will find this book full of real stories from missionaries who have faced the same obstacles that were written on the Wall at Urbana. The writer of Ecclesiastes tells us that "There is nothing new under the sun" (Ecclesiastes 1:9), and that appears to be true of the types of obstacles that get in the way of people going into missions. Some of these stories come from men and women new to the mission field, some in their first or second year of service. Others come from people who have been missionaries for decades but who faced many of the same obstacles written on the Wall.

Each chapter begins where this book began—with the Urbana Wall. Each will address a particular obstacle, with actual quotes from the Wall. Then we will read the stories of missionaries who faced that obstacle and experienced God's faithfulness in helping them to scale the wall before them, to reach the goal He had placed in their hearts.

As I read these stories, I was reminded how God works with each of us as unique individuals. No story is like anyone else's story. God's answer to one person's dilemma was very different from what He led another to do in a similar situation. That is why I have included multiple stories in each chapter. We cannot expect God to do for us exactly what He did for someone else, but we can expect Him to do something amazing on our behalf—something that fits His plan for us and is custom-made for our situation.

At the end of each chapter you will find more quotes from the Wall, but these are slightly different. As I was sorting through the quotes for each chapter, I realized that some were just expressions of the limitations they were facing, just lists of the troublesome obstacles. But others were heartfelt prayers of dedication and petitions for help in overcoming these obstacles. I felt these were a fitting end to each chapter after we have heard the stories of those who experienced God's faithful help. These stories give us encouragement to cry out to our Lord to help us as we face the obstacles before us. Perhaps these prayers from the Wall will echo the desire of your heart.

I realize that the obstacle you are facing might not be included in this book. I chose the ones that were listed at least a few times, but your obstacle may be as unique as the person God created you to be. I believe that you will be encouraged to see that God can overcome any obstacle in your life, just as He has for others in the stories you will be reading. We have a powerful and creative God who is looking to work wonders in the lives of those who trust Him. "For the eyes of the LORD move to and fro throughout the earth that He may strongly support those whose heart is completely His" (2 Chronicles 16:9).

If you think God might be calling you to serve Him in missions, read on—but be careful! The stories ahead could lead to inspiration, motivation, and enough of a boost to your faith to allow you to trust Him to help you scale that wall in front of you.

PART TWO:
FACING OUR WALL
OF OBSTACLES

FEARS

PERSONAL DESIRES

RELATIONSHIPS

SPIRITUAL INADEQUACY

PREPARATION ISSUES

3

General Fear

Father, I offer you these things that might limit me from doing my part in seeing the nations worship you . . .

"Fear of unsanitary conditions, AIDS, weird food, strange places, not having a comfortable life, and losing my relationship with my boyfriend."

"Fear of rejection, fear of loneliness, fear of singleness, fear of helplessness, fear of inadequate faith and power."

"Fear of associating with distasteful people."

"Fear is my greatest obstacle. What am I so afraid of? We are afraid of being hurt, our psyche is really weak, but Jesus has been hurt for us. With His cross we bear our own cross too. My hope is that Your salvation is always enough for me."

"Fear, doubt, rebellion, and uncertainty. However, let me say that God is absolutely amazing in that He is strengthening me and guiding me in and through His perfect love and blessed promises. 'Perfect love casts out all fear.'"

The obstacle that most often appeared on the Wall was fear. Half of the responses mentioned some type of fear. Specific fears that showed up most often have been given their own chapters: fear of an uncertain future and fear of what others will think. Many mentioned a variety of fears or just fear in general.

Fear is a natural reaction to dangerous situations, and it helps to keep us safe by causing us to avoid harm. But fear can also keep us from doing things that we should do, that God wants us to do. We need His wisdom and guidance to discern when He is asking us to trust Him and act in spite of our fears. When we obey Him, He promises, "For I am the LORD your God, who upholds your right hand, Who says to you, 'Do not fear, I will help you'" (Isaiah 41:13).

Sometimes our fears are of what we know we will face, such as raising support, living in a new culture, or exposing ourselves to possible physical or health dangers. But often our fears are of the unknown—the uncertainty of whether we will be successful, how people will react to us, and what we will actually be expected to do if we commit ourselves.

If we are honest, we will realize that all of our fears stem from a lack of faith in God's willingness to help us. We are not sure we can really trust Him with total control of our lives. But that is what the life of faith is about—stepping out into the unknown while trusting God with our lives.

"John" and "Jody" are Americans who moved past their fears when they felt God calling them to serve in Afghanistan and, once there, found God to be very faithful in the midst of a very fearful situation:

We had good jobs but were restless in our hearts. We wondered if there might be a place somewhere where our skills could be used in missions. I (Jody) have been in clerical work most of my life, and John has been a design draftsman for farm machinery for over thirty years. As we looked into the possibilities, we were connected to a man who worked in South Asia for an agency that serves the people in Afghanistan in practical ways as a means of showing God's love.

We visited one country for two weeks and were very impressed with what different organizations were doing there. John was able to visit the work of this particular service agency in Afghanistan and was again impressed. We decided that if there was an opening for us we would like to serve there.

As we progressed through the application process, we were often asked questions like:

1) Why, at age sixty, would you want to go to a Third World country . . . and Afghanistan of all places? Aren't you afraid?
2) Why would you walk away from job security and the routine of work?
3) Why would you leave the security of home and family . . . at your age?

During this time of uncertainty, questioning, and support raising a particular verse became very important to me:

> Fear not; [there is nothing to fear] for I am with you; do not look around you in terror and be dismayed, for I am your God. I will strengthen and harden you to difficulties; yes, I will help you; yes, I will hold you up and retain you with My [victorious] right hand of righteousness and justice. (Isaiah 41:10, Amplified)

I posted this verse in my cubicle at work where I could see it everyday. I posted it on the monitor of our computer at home where it could be seen often. This verse helped to answer those questions and calm my fears.

On January 8, 2001, we left to begin our work in Afghanistan. We had the privilege of trying to learn the language of Dari, establishing a new facility, and working as the personnel coordinator until August 30.

At 10 PM, long after we had gone to bed on that very hot day, there was a persistent knock at the door. Our *chowkidar* (a watchman who protects the house and watches the gate) whispered to John that Taliban were at the gate. There were, in fact, three pickup truckloads of armed Taliban outside, with a group walking up the driveway, when John stepped outside to greet them. Seven of them entered our home and politely but firmly asked for all of our communication systems (a satellite phone and ham radio) and told us that we were under house arrest. Two armed Taliban would serve as guards at our gate, and we were not to leave the compound nor attempt to communicate with anyone.

They left thirty minutes later, leaving the two guards with a couple of cots to sleep on.

John went down a few minutes later, taking the guards and the *chowkidar* each a bottle of ice-cold water for the night. We fed them the next day and a half and kept them refreshed with hot green tea and cold water. Two of our female team members were brought to our home on Friday with their luggage to stay the night. The following morning our director was brought with his luggage. We learned that all our offices and homes were sealed. We were put into our van, along with Taliban, and were escorted out of town to the Afghan-Pakistan border where we had to walk across with only the possessions we could carry.

We were very surprised to be met at the border by journalists and photographers, and we learned from them that there had been an order from Khandahar that all the Christian NGOs (Non-Governmental Organizations, like ours) had to be out of the country that very day. We were the first out. We were very grateful that none of us were hurt or harassed.

We have since learned that most of our things were looted, stolen, gone. The offices, the guesthouse, and our personal homes are no longer available to us, and their furnishings and documents are gone. Following the 9/11 attack on the United States, we were evacuated to Germany where we all met together as a team to determine what our next steps should be. Everyone felt that we should regroup and continue the work of our Lord through this service organization. Plans were established, and we all left for our home countries to explain to our supporters what had happened.

Does God keep His word? Previous to our expulsion, we had been in Kabul when Dayna Curry and Heather Mercer failed to show up at their homes at the end of the day. We learned that they, and then the rest of the SNI team, including their Afghan staff, were arrested. A Scripture became special to me that day in August when we returned to the city, Psalm 94:20–23:

Can a corrupt throne be allied with you—one that brings on misery by its decrees? They band together against the righteous and condemn the innocent to death. But the LORD has become my fortress, and my God the rock in whom I take refuge. He will repay them for their sins and destroy them for their wickedness; the LORD our God will destroy them. (NIV)

All those who were arrested have since come out alive and well, and the Taliban government has been defeated.

The fears that we felt regarding our jobs, home, family, financial support, age, usefulness—and then when the Taliban came and took away our freedom and material possessions—these fears were all swallowed up in the words "fear not." God indeed strengthened us and helped us in our times of need.

Not only did God strengthen and help them with their fears during their ordeal but He also allowed them to overcome any fears about going back. Several months after they were forced to leave, John, Jody, and the rest of their team were back in Afghanistan setting up their homes and restarting the projects they had been forced to abandon.

God is faithful to care for His people even in fearful situations. Jesus said, "Peace I leave with you; My peace I give to you; not as the world gives do I give to you. Do not let your heart be troubled, nor let it be fearful" (John 14:27).

Sometimes God uses persecution and even the death of His people to further His purposes. Throughout history doors have been opened and people have been inspired through the sacrifice of those who have given their lives for the cause of Christ—people like Jim Elliott and Nate Saint and their companions, whose deaths opened up a people group to the gospel and inspired many to follow their example into missions.

On November 21, 2002, Bonnie Witherall became a martyr for Christ when her life was suddenly taken by an unknown gunman who entered the prenatal clinic early that morning. Bonnie was preparing tea and cookies for the Palestinian refugee women that would be cared for that morning. She delighted in showing mercy and kindness to these Arab women and sharing the love of Jesus with them whenever she could.

Just a few months before her death, some friends visited Bonnie and her husband, Gary, where they lived and worked as missionaries in Sidon, Lebanon. They interviewed Bonnie on video, and she shared about her struggle with fear and how the Lord and her husband helped her to overcome it. Here are Bonnie's own words:

On September 11 I came home from the clinic so excited because that day I had had two or three opportunities to tell people about Jesus. I was so fired up. I felt as though I had a purpose here and things were really great. Then I turned on the news, and I saw it—I saw it live from here, because it was four or five o'clock, which means it was about nine in the morning there. I couldn't believe it, and like all Americans I was in a state of shock. But we had a little bit different perspective, because I had just spent the whole day talking with and loving these Arab women, showing them mercy and kindness; and that night they were rejoicing in the Palestinian camp that this had happened in America!

For us the real challenge was how to love these people who you just really, honestly wanted to hate! You can't fathom how much I just wanted to turn my back on them and go back home. I couldn't understand these people who would rejoice so much over such loss and pain—especially people who had endured so much pain and loss themselves. That was a real spiritual challenge for me, to get the resources from the Lord to love these people who were so filled with joy over the loss in the United States.

That first two weeks I didn't go out very much. I didn't know if it was safe. I felt like everyone was looking at me and knew I was an American. I felt like I was a target for everybody. I was really fearful and really ready, not to go home, but definitely ready to go to Beirut. Sidon is a lot more conservative and fundamental than Beirut.

I remember talking to my husband, Gary, one night. I was in tears and trembling, and I said, "I can't handle it—I can't live like this." Gary said to me, "Bonnie, there is nothing you can do to add a day to your life, and there is nothing you can do to take away one day." He helped me to see that every one of my days is written in God's plan, and I can't do anything to change that. After he said this I felt a release from this fear and a sense of freedom to be able to walk down the streets of Sidon, to be able to talk about Jesus, to be bolder than I ever have been before, because I don't know how long we will have here in Sidon. I don't know how long we will be able to tell people about Jesus. I don't want something like September 11 to put so much fear in me that I am disabled from doing what I've been called to do. So I feel I've come a long way, and now I don't have fear in that same way.

I still have fears about other things—obviously I have a lot of issues in my life that God is still working on—but as far as the terrorism/September 11 issues, no, I'm not scared. I know that God has my life in His hands and that I am where He wants me to be right now. I'm confident of that, and I'm happy to be here.

One more thing to remember is that every Arab that I've met on the street has been very kind to me. I just want to tell people to make friends with Arabs. They are wonderful people. I feel so blessed and so honored to be in this part of the world—even after September 11. I honestly wouldn't have wanted to be anywhere else, and I count it a privilege and a joy to be in the Middle East.

It's not always easy, and it's obviously hard to live in an uncertain place. You can't really put down roots, because you never know when you'll have to leave or be evacuated and things will spiral out of control. But I feel honored to know and to love Arabs, to eat and fellowship with them. I've really learned a lot, because I had no idea before I came! I had no Arab friends and no Muslim friends. I was scared as anything to go to the Muslim world. I had said to the Lord, "I am never going to the Middle East. You can send me anywhere You want, but I'm not going to go there." Until you expose yourself, it's very normal and natural for you to have those feelings, but I feel blessed that God called me here so that my views could change and I could experience what it is like to be friends with Arab people.

Bonnie is now in heaven, where she no longer has to deal with issues like fear—but what about her husband Gary? How has all this affected his faith, his ministry, and his life? I asked him those very things, and here is his response:

Bonnie was my best friend. We fell in love and enjoyed being with each other. We shared our joys, experiences, and pain with each other. To know she is gone is devastation. My close friend is no longer there to share the road of life with me. I feel that everything is gone, and I have been thrown onto the Lord. The Lord has drawn close to me. I have fallen into His arms. He sustains me. He has comforted me, and I have survived in His presence. The pain of this tragedy is so enormous, yet the presence of God in my life has given peace.

It seems I am so alone, and yet the Lord's arms are around me, as I believe they are around Bonnie. I can do nothing other than trust with everything that is within me. Bonnie, my greatest treasure in life, is worthy of handing to Jesus, because what He has done for me is so great.

God prepared both of us for this tragedy. We both often talked about holding things and each other loosely. In doing this we were able to be living sacrifices. We were willing to even lay down our lives for the kingdom. It is a life where Christ comes first. But this is a day-today thing. It is not a place you arrive. There is only today, and one cannot know what tomorrow will hold.

Fear and boldness are two words that are closely related. Fear is like oil that seeps into all the places of your life. It needs to be dealt with and renounced. Boldness comes to replace it. For what are you ready to lay down your precious life or the life of the one you love? This is a question that the American churches do not face. But in many places in the world, it is a daily reality that must be considered. I would rather burn brightly for Christ with risks than live a meaningless existence in a place regarded as safe. The safest place to be is where Jesus leads you, doing whatever He tells you to do—just ask Jonah.

The impact of Bonnie's death has been nothing short of stunning. As I share our story, I see how people are moved to deeper commitment and a willingness to serve. God's work through this situation silences me. I can do nothing except sit back and allow God to reign. I hope that thousands will respond to the life and death of Bonnie and *go*. Who will go to these lost fields where the costs can be so high? Lord, raise up men and women of faith!

Bonnie and Gary are wonderful examples of overcoming fear and being willing to do whatever God asks. Gary was able to encourage Bonnie past her fear after 9/11 with the truth found in Psalm 139:16: "You saw me before I was born. Every day of my life was recorded in your book. Every moment was laid out before a single day had passed" (NLT). Bonnie's death was not a tragic accident but part of God's plan for her and Gary's ministry. While this is not what Gary would have chosen, he has found the Lord sufficient to help him through this, and faithful to use it in meaningful and effective ways to further God's kingdom—which is what Bonnie's life was and Gary's life still is all about.

"Lord, is it fear in my life? Help me to remember that You are greater than my fear."

"Dear God, I lift up my fear that hinders me from giving my time to go to the mission field. May You make me a servant wherever You lead me."

"May we remember that we who are in You are greater than he who is in the world."

"Take away my life. I lay it in Your hands. Guide my heart and take my fears. Please take care of my mom!"

"Forgive me for not sharing my faith as You would have me do. I give You my fears and troubles—give me strength my precious Father. You shed Your blood for me."

"Lord, intimidation comes to mind as I think of what is holding me back but of what? I ask to behold people according to Your love, not with fear."

"Father God, I offer my fears, my loneliness, my worries, and my troublesome heart. I love You, and I wait on You patiently."

"God, I give You my pride, my fear, my doubt. You alone hold the days of my life. God I'm scared of language barriers and of things that are different. I am afraid of going there alone, but I chose to praise You. Do with me, weak though I am, what You will. I give You my life today."

"Be anxious for nothing, but in everything by prayer and supplication with thanksgiving let your requests be made known to God. And the peace of God, which surpasses all comprehension, will guard your hearts and your minds in Christ Jesus" (Philippians 4:6–7).

4

Fear of an Uncertain Future

$\mathbf{F}$ather, I offer you these things that might limit me from doing my part in seeing the nations worship you . . .

"Fear of the unknown."

"Fear of the future—my grip on the past."

"Fear of not knowing what awesome plans You have in store for me."

"Fear of something different, too small of a vision."

"My desire for security . . . as if I could trust myself!"

"My fears of the unknown, my lack of trust with the future, the uncertainty of the future, my comfort zone, my pride . . . Oh Lord! It's too much but praise Jesus."

It's interesting that many of us believe that letting God determine our future makes it more uncertain than if we make our own plans. If we took a survey of elderly people and asked, "Did your life turn out the way you planned or expected?" most would say that their lives included many unforeseen twists and turns. Most of what happens to us is out of our control—so why do we think that trusting our life to God, who is all-knowing and all-powerful, is something to be feared, or somehow less stable? Actually, if we really think about it, God is ultimately in control of our lives anyway, and we benefit if we acknowledge that fact and decide to cooperate with His plans. Proverbs 16:9 teaches us that "The mind of man plans his way, But the LORD directs his steps."

I believe that the main issue at stake here is the belief that if we let God choose, He will make us do things we don't want to do—things too hard, too scary, or too dangerous. Do we really believe that God is good? Trustworthy? Able to take care of all our needs? If not, we have reason to worry about the future. But if He is all this, and more, our future is in good hands. There is a reassuring promise for us in Jeremiah 29:11: "'For I know the plans that I have for you,' declares the LORD, 'plans for welfare and not for calamity to give you a future and a hope.'"

Rebecca, from the United States, found herself at a crossroads in her career and was challenged to take a step out of her job and into an uncertain future. A suggestion that came "out of the blue" from her pastor sounded unrealistic at first, but she eventually recognized it as the voice of God asking her to trust Him with her future.

At thirty-seven years of age I thought I was finally settled into the business world after years of climbing the career ladder. I'd never considered going on a missions trip, let alone becoming a missionary. Amazing how God works His will into our lives when we're not looking!

I found myself growing increasingly frustrated and dissatisfied with corporate America. After working over a dozen years in the Washington, D.C., area in various forms of communications and public relations, with inhuman demands and little reward, I was burnt out—mentally, emotionally, physically, and spiritually. Even though I was in a very promising job in a fast-growing company in the nation's capital, I was unmotivated, uncaring about my job performance, and unsure what to do about it.

Fortunately, I have a wonderful relationship with my pastor and his wife, who were concerned enough to spend some extended time with me. After hearing me complain and fret about my lot in life, Jeff, my pastor, asked me if I thought that God was asking me to quit my job. As a single woman with a mortgage, credit card bills, car payments, and other financial obligations, the idea seemed ridiculous. I knew I'd be able to pay my bills on my sparkling personality and stunning good looks for only so long! Living in the Washington, D.C., area was wonderful, but it was expensive. I wasn't considering leaving the business world; I just thought I needed a new job.

I also have a wonderful sister, who has served as a professional mentor during my career. From a business perspective, she knew I was so burnt out that I wouldn't be able to get a new job even if I wanted it. She said that my spirit, attitude, and desire were all so broken that I wouldn't be able to hide it in a job interview, and she was right.

So I knew Pastor Jeff's suggestion was probably the only viable option for me, but from a worldly perspective it didn't make sense. I didn't know how I could explain to my family, friends, coworkers, or my boss about quitting a "great" job without having a new job. That would make my future too uncertain. But I knew deep down in my heart that it was *exactly* what God was calling me to do.

I wrestled with this decision for about a month. I prayed over and over about other options, but God kept closing the door on anything else, other than quitting without a job.

I finally submitted my resignation, much to my boss's displeasure and surprise, but I did so confidently, knowing that God was in control. Almost immediately after submitting my resignation, my boss offered me a consultant arrangement, which I accepted on the spot. Instantaneously, God provided the financial means to meet my obligations but released me from the daily pressure of the job.

About this time my church was planning a short-term mission trip to Albania. Shortly after leaving my job, Jeff asked me to pray about going on the mission trip. My first thought was no, but then after thinking and praying about it, I couldn't come up with a good reason not to. Since I was now a consultant I could adjust my work schedule without any problems. And the church was covering most of the cost of the trip, so there weren't financial considerations. I have to admit that I really didn't pray about it much because it seemed like a no-brainer. Why not go? What could it hurt? So I said yes, not having any idea that such a small, seemingly insignificant decision would later lead to a huge change in my life.

I loved my time in Albania, which really surprised me. I didn't experience jetlag or culture shock, and I adjusted easily to the missionary lifestyle.

More importantly, I was very moved and convicted by the fact that I'd never really seen God as the God of the entire world but had boxed Him in to the United States. I realized that I honestly had no view of world missions beyond listening to mission trip reports at my church or reading the occasional prayer letter from my overseas missionary friends. I thought God wanted me to come to Albania just to broaden my mind about world missions—and I was excited about that. I knew I could go back home and share with everyone that God is really God of all, not just the United States. I was excited to finally realize God's purpose for leading me to Albania.

However, while there I met a recruiter for the mission agency that was organizing our trip. I initially wasn't interested in talking with her, but I was curious about how one "recruits" missionaries. I'd always thought missionaries were "called" to a particular country or that they had had a passion to be a missionary since they were children. I've never felt called or had that passion, so I was skeptical, but the Lord piqued my curiosity somewhat. Then a friend encouraged me by saying, "What could it hurt?" so I met with her.

I'd told the Lord I'd be open to whatever He was doing in my life, but inside I was *sure* He wasn't asking me to become a missionary! The position I initially discussed with the recruiter wasn't a good fit for me, and, boy, was I relieved! I literally leaned back in my seat and said to the Lord, "Okay, Lord, I pursued this, but it's not right. Thanks."

She and I talked a little more about my background and career. When I mentioned that I had a degree in journalism and that my entire career had been in the communications/publications arena, her eyes lit up. She mentioned a communications role in Hungary, and as soon as she said *Hungary* something clicked inside. I was instantly interested. I know this could only come from the Lord, because I have never been interested in leaving my friends and family and moving halfway across the world to become a missionary! And, I never had any interest in Hungary—I wasn't even sure I could find it on the map!

Within a week of the trip, I had an e-mail from the head of the Hungary office indicating an interest in talking with me. I was very excited to pursue this opportunity and prayed that I'd be open to whatever the Lord was doing in my life. Providentially, I had already planned a vacation to Europe in the fall with my mom and sister. So the three of us went to Budapest in October, and I interviewed for the position. After returning to the United States and praying and talking with trusted friends, I knew that the Lord was leading me to at least a two-year stint with this team. I made a commitment to go and a year later arrived in Hungary. When it became clear that the Lord was calling me to leave my job, I committed my life to whatever or wherever He was leading me. Though that made my future uncertain, I wanted to be faithful to what He was doing. I never dreamed it would be missions, but it undoubtedly was

His plan for me. If I hadn't left my job, I wouldn't have gone on the missions trip to Albania, wouldn't have met and talked to the recruiter, wouldn't have heard about the position in Hungary, and wouldn't now be serving Him on the field. Isn't it so cool how God orchestrates our lives perfectly if we are only open to it?

Since joining God on the mission field, He has lead me to a place—physically, spiritually, and emotionally— where I have only Him to trust and depend on. My relationship with the Lord has grown stronger and more confident, as He has shown me consistently that He is the way, the truth, and the life. While I have kicked and screamed at times, He always returns my questions, frustrations, and, occasionally, my willingness to obey with love, assurance, and blessings.

Rebecca has learned that trusting God with her future has led her in ways and to places she would never have expected. In addition to finding purpose and joy in serving Him, she has realized the added benefits of a deeper knowledge of God and a stronger faith in Him. There's nothing like total dependence on God to help you realize that He is indeed faithful and all we really need.

Susan, a graduate student from Canada, had an interest in missions but no conviction about where to serve. Even when she thought she had it figured out, the Lord surprised her by changing her plans to line up with His—but not without a struggle.

For years I had been interested in missions, but I never knew what to do beyond that. I would hear people say things like, "Ever since I was five years old I knew that one day I would be going to China." I would listen and think, "Wow, that's great, but I'd have no idea where to go. And, after all, you can't just call up a missions office and say, 'I want to be a missionary, but I have no clue where,' can you?" (I know now that you actually can.)

I was working on a master's degree in Belfast, Northern Ireland, and one evening the founder of a mission organization came to speak at the Christian Union group at the university. His opening words riveted me. "I think it's awful how we in the West live when two-thirds of the people on this earth are going to bed tonight hungry." You could have heard a pin drop. He went on. "And tonight is not going to be some nice 'consider missions' talk." I thought, "Great!" because I do consider missions and don't know what to do from there. "I'm here to challenge each and every one of you to think and pray about doing two years overseas, either with my organization or some other group. That won't be all of you here, but it'll be a lot more of you than you think."

That is when the feeling started in the back of my neck—the certainty that I was one of the people that he was talking about. In a few months I would finish my degree. I didn't have a job yet. I wasn't married, so I didn't have a spouse's career and interests to consider. But where did I go from there?

He continued, "If you don't know which place is the place for you, just push on doors to see if they will open."

Right. So making it very clear that God could change any of the details, I decided that I would pursue serving with this man's organization overseas for two years. As I was trying to determine where I should serve, I experienced a three-week trip to North Africa that greatly impacted me. I discovered that there is a support base in Spain that helps to facilitate the work in North Africa. That sounded just right.

I set things in motion to join this group as soon as I got back from Belfast, and the people in Spain were happy that I wanted to join their team. But then God spoke to me. God hardly ever "speaks" to me in a really direct, unmistakable way—maybe four times in my life, total—but this was one of them.

God said, "Susan, you're not going to Spain."

I couldn't believe it! *Hello?*—the 10/40 Window? Huge need? But of course God is God, so He knows all about the 10/40 Window.

So if not Spain, where?

"The Canadian home office."

Join this great, cutting-edge mission organization to stay not only in my home country but also in my home province? Office work? No way! So being confident that there was no way God could do this, I prayed that if He could *show* me and *convince* me that Canada was the place for me to be, then I would stay in Canada and serve in the home office. And He did just that, because He is big and He always wins.

Two things hit me hard:

First, a sermon. I can't remember much of it, but I clearly remember that the preacher paused and looked at us all. He said, "If anything is becoming more important to you than God, even if it's a desire to serve Him, that thing is an idol in your life." The word *idol* slammed into my head. I realized that my desire to serve God overseas had become more important to me than being where God wanted me to be. I repented.

Second, God brought to mind a passage, 1 Kings 19:14–18. Elijah, having just destroyed the prophets of Baal, is running for his life from Queen Jezebel and is really tired and scared. He basically says to God, "I don't want to do it Your way, and You don't have any choice because I'm the only one left who serves You." God replied, "I have reserved 7,000 in Israel who are faithful and loyal to me." The message for me was clear—ministry in the 10/40 Window would not cease because I would not be going there. My life and what I do with my life, matters very much to God. But in another way, it does not make one bit of difference where I am or what I am doing. God's purposes will be performed, with or without me.

So Canada it would be.

My first introductory prayer letters had been all about what I had hoped to do in Spain. Now I had the task of writing to my supporters and saying, "I'm not going to Spain. I'm staying in Canada. Do you still think I'm a missionary?" That was one of the most difficult letters I have ever had to write. I don't think *I* was convinced that I would still be a missionary in that job, but I knew I needed to obey God.

Raising support felt like a huge mountain to climb. The few people who had already started to support me financially made it clear that they would continue to do so, which was a confirmation and also a relief.

As the finances started coming together, other issues were coming to the surface. I have always had the fear that if I gave my life completely to God and really surrendered, He would put me in a situation that would be difficult and unpleasant. Whenever I was in a meeting and the preacher called for people to give everything to God, I would always give what I could and admit to God that I wasn't yet able to let go of it all. The first time I really surrendered I was intensely scared. But somehow I was able to do it anyway, through His help and grace.

I have worked for this mission organization for more than six years now, starting with the short-term trip to Morocco, then three years in Canada, and now three years at a training center in England. As with all of us (even those who have a blueprint for the next ten years), my future is still uncertain.

After years of being single, the Lord has blessed me with a boyfriend. My boyfriend comes from a different continent than I do, and now he is living and working in his home country. A few months from now I might be working with the same mission agency, but in *his* home country with a new culture and a new language to learn. And I am taking these steps of faith without a guarantee that things will work out between us. (We are both sure that we want to marry each other one day, but we acknowledge that we belong to God, and He has the option to do whatever He wants with our lives.)

My time in missions has given me example after example of God proving Himself faithful to me. Many of these lessons I perhaps couldn't have learned at home. I am not a masochist; I am not looking for maximum difficulty and challenge in my life. I am someone who is easily made anxious and would secretly like a nice, well-ordered, predictable life but who has just enough God-given courage to act on the fact that that is just not reality.

The thought of the next ten years scares me. The thought of the next twenty-four hours doesn't. Maybe, one day at a time, I can serve God my whole life, *with* my whole life, whether in missions or in some other way. Maybe, one day at a time, I can continue to prove that Jesus is faithful. For all of us, it is His grace that gets us through life, one day at a time.

Susan has given us a good reminder that although we can sometimes make long-term plans, we always need to serve God day-by-day, being open to His leading and redirecting of our path. We can't foresee the future, but the good news is that He can and will guide us and provide for us accordingly, if we let Him. Our future may seem uncertain to us, but not to Him. If He is trustworthy (and He is), then allowing Him to determine our future is nothing to fear.

"Lord, help me with fear of the unknown to come, that I may fully trust You for my everything!"

"Father, I give up my life to You and all I struggle with—the fear of the unknown—but I have my trust in You."

"Concern for my future. Father, it's in Your hands—whatever my future holds."

"Father, I love You. I give You my all, and I also give You control of my future—do as You will. I want to follow Your son, Jesus."

"God I offer up my life and my FEAR and

uncertainty about the future. Take it—I want to serve You!"

"And we know that God causes all things to work together for good to those who love God, to those who are called according to His purpose" (Romans 8:28).

"Do not worry then, saying, 'What will we eat?' or 'What will we drink?' or 'What will we wear for clothing? For the Gentiles eagerly seek all these things; for your heavenly Father knows that you need all these things. But seek first His kingdom and His righteousness, and all these things will be added to you. So do not worry about tomorrow; for tomorrow will care for itself. Each day has enough trouble of its own" (Matthew 6:31–34).

5

Fear of What Others Think

Father, I offer you these things that might limit me from doing my part in seeing the nations worship you . . .

"Fear of what people think."

"What others think, especially my peers at school. Caring about how people/friends will react to a radical Christian."

"My insecurities and fears about being rejected by others."

"Fear and uncertainty in doing God's will. Trying to please others instead of God and being too concerned with myself instead of others."

"Giving my will over to God's will and losing my pride."

"My need to please others ahead of pleasing You."

"My reputation."

"Fear of self-consciousness and what others may think."

"Expectations."

"Fear of rejection, being met with hostility, not being accepted, being looked down upon."

———————————

As I tabulated the responses from the wall and put them into categories, I found the kinds of things the students were afraid of to be very interesting. Very few listed issues of physical safety, health, or suffering as the focus of their fears. Of the things specifically mentioned, the biggest category had to do with what other people would think of them, pride, and fear of rejection.

Many of us are very sensitive about other people's opinions of us. We often admire people who live their lives according to their convictions in spite of what is socially acceptable, because it takes courage to do so and is relatively rare these days. We fear being labeled "close minded," "narrow thinking," or, worst of all, "politically incorrect"! In this day of ultra tolerance, to say that our beliefs are right and others are wrong is socially unacceptable, but that is just what Christ asked us to do.

In Matthew 28:19–20 He commands us to "Go therefore and make disciples of all the nations, baptizing them in the name of the Father and the Son and the Holy Spirit, teaching them to observe all that I commanded you." And making disciples involves teaching Christ's own statement in John 14:6: "I am the way, and the truth, and the life; no one comes to the Father but through Me." We are called to be narrow thinkers—narrow in the sense that we believe what the Bible teaches about God and salvation, not accepting other religions as valid options. But that will bring us criticism. We *will* look foolish to those with a broader, more inclusive outlook—but then, God planned it that way.

Paul explains in 1 Corinthians 1:17–27:

For Christ didn't send me to baptize, but to preach the Good News—and not with clever speeches and high-sounding ideas, for fear that the cross of Christ would lose its power. I know very well how foolish the message of the cross sounds to those who are on the road to destruction. But we who are being saved recognize this message as the very power of God. As the Scriptures say, "I will destroy human wisdom and discard their most brilliant ideas." So where does this leave the philosophers, the scholars, and the world's brilliant debaters? God has made them all look foolish and has shown their wisdom to be useless nonsense. Since God in his wisdom saw to it that the world would never find him through human wisdom, he has used our foolish preaching to save all who believe. God's way seems foolish to the Jews because they want a sign from heaven to prove it is true. And it is foolish to the Greeks because they believe only what agrees with their own wisdom. So when we preach that Christ was crucified, the Jews are offended, and the Gentiles say it's all nonsense. But to those called by God to salvation, both Jews and Gentiles, Christ is the mighty power of God and the wonderful wisdom of God. This "foolish" plan of God is far wiser than the wisest of human plans, and God's weakness is far stronger than the greatest of human strength. Remember, dear brothers and sisters, that few of you were wise in the world's eyes, or powerful, or wealthy when God called you. Instead, God deliberately chose things the world considers foolish in order to shame those who think they are wise. And he chose those who are powerless to shame those who are powerful. (NLT)

Getting past the fear of what others think means being willing to look foolish, narrow minded, or radical. It means wanting to please God more than wanting to please other people, caring more about what He thinks of us than what others think.

Mike grew up near London, England, in a family with certain religious expectations. He had to choose between doing what others felt was right and respectable and what he knew God was asking him to do. Once he got past fearing what others would think, God was able to use him (for thirty-five years so far!) in places like India, Pakistan, and Nepal.

I came to Christ at the University of Dublin in 1962. It was a radical moment in my life, and it gave me a whole new perspective on the future. I guess the nature of the change stemmed from the kind of person I was brought up to be, which suddenly stood in stark contrast to the kind of person I sensed God wanted me to be.

I was brought up in a good, stable, middle-class home with a strong Anglican (Episcopalian) tradition. My grandfather was a high-church vicar and my mother a confirmed churchgoer, so I was taught the obligations and expectations of the church, was confirmed, and was taken to communion. The community I was raised in basically believed that religion was good for society, but too much enthusiasm or passion was to be abhorred.

My mother was a strong-willed woman whom I respected and loved, but I lived in the shadow of her strong personality. I wanted to please her and have her think well of me. When I came to Christ while away from home at university a number of things took on a new perspective.

First, I was astounded to discover that I could be sure of my salvation—it depended on God's promise and not on my weak and erratic faith. My mother had told me something different and now argued against my newfound certainty.

Second, I was excited. The gospel became relevant not only for me and my future but also for the whole world. To pass it on, to see others saved, to give my life for the spread of Christian Truth—all this became a high priority instead of something you only do on Sunday. The gospel became more important than respectability, and my mother found this hard to understand. She felt my passion for the spread of the gospel bordered on a fanaticism that was not acceptable and was becoming an embarrassment to her.

Third, though I was saved through an Episcopalian minister—Reverend John Stott, a well-known evangelical—and attended an Anglican church in Dublin, I was soon going to the Baptist church and sometimes to a rather offbeat semi-Brethren assembly. Then, after graduation, I applied to go to a Brethren Bible school. I did not tell my mother when I was baptized in the sea by the Brethren—that would have been too hard for her to accept!

My mother was horrified by my choices. Her image of me as a respectable minister in the established church evaporated. She began to object to the direction I was moving in. At no point did she ever dig in her heels and refuse to allow me to do what I felt was right—her objections reached me through hints, innuendo, and argument. I guess her stubbornness only strengthened my conviction and determination not to be influenced by her (perhaps a degree of carnal independence typical of post-teenagers, but it surely served God's plan for me).

In the end I stuck to what I knew to be right—a kind of spiritual stubbornness, without which I could have quickly been diverted to a more respectable and "sensible" life course. But I would have missed God's plan to use me overseas. In due time my mother came to accept that God was leading me. She was changing too. In fact, after I graduated from Bible school, joined the mission, and left for India, she became my greatest financial and prayer supporter.

Mike found out that by sticking to what he knew was the right thing to do, he was able to obey God and, eventually, see his mother's opinions change. So often the people whose opinions we are most influenced by are our parents, who are also influenced by how others will view them because of what their children do. Many missionaries have found that once they make their commitments and follow through, their parents and others who were initially concerned see the value of what they are doing, see God's leading and provision in their lives, and come to respect and even support them in their ministry.

Bärbel, from Austria, found herself struggling with what both her parents and her friends at work would say about her interest in missions. She actually found that she misjudged what her father would think and was surprised by his reaction. Her friends at work, although unable to understand exactly why she would choose to serve in missions, saw the reality of her faith and commitment to God, which she couldn't communicate as effectively through conversations around the office.

After seven years of studying technical mathematics and insurance mathematics, I got a job with a company that works on pension plans for other companies. Although it sounds a bit boring, I loved my job. I really had a lot of fun with my coworkers who all were around my age.

In spite of the enjoyment I felt at work, I came to a point where I thought there must be more to the Christian life than what I was experiencing. From reading my Bible and other books, I got the impression that something was missing. About this time I attended a mission conference and learned about an interesting opportunity to serve. My first thought was that I could go for two months during the summer, when my workload is lighter and I could easily get away from work.

I thought that spending time in a new environment would help me to become more dependent on God and to grow spiritually. So I asked a lot of questions and found out that two months was not long enough—I would have to make a two-year commitment! When I heard this my immediate reaction was "Forget it then! I won't quit my job for that. My job is too good to give up. Besides, what would my dad, who paid for my studies for seven years, say? I have only been working for three years. He is not a Christian and would probably think that he invested his money in vain." I especially thought he wouldn't like the fact that I needed to raise support, because he values independence.

But I could not get the ministry opportunity off my mind. After struggling with this for a while I realized that God says in His Word, "And everyone who has left houses or brothers or sisters or father or mother or children or farms for My name's sake, will receive many times as much, and will inherit eternal life" (Matthew 19:29). Since *farm* refers to a person's livelihood, I thought that if it were God's will that I quit my job for Him, He could give me an even better job after my missions commitment was over! From then on I was able to let go of my job mentally, and I actually started seeing some negative things about my job.

But I still couldn't decide. I evaluated my motives. Did I expect a better relationship with God? I realized that the busy lifestyle of this ministry would actually be a challenge to my spiritual growth. Did I want to travel? No, seeing new places was not particularly exciting for me. Somehow I realized that God had put this idea in my heart, and the only reason I would go was out of obedience to Him.

I still was not sure. My family and many of my friends are not Christians, so I wanted to be certain that this was God's desire for me and not just my own idea. I knew that I would have a lot of discussions with all these people, and I didn't want them to talk me out of it by saying it is a strange idea or that I am crazy. I was concerned about what they would think of me.

So I prayed about it and asked God to speak to me clearly. He led me to Luke 10:2–3, "And He was saying to them, 'The harvest is plentiful, but the laborers are few; therefore beseech the Lord of the harvest to send out laborers into His harvest. Go your ways; behold, I send you out as lambs in the midst of wolves.'" I believed that God was clearly saying that He wanted me to go.

For a variety of reasons, I decided to join eighteen months later. This time of waiting gave my family a chance to get used to the fact that I would be leaving for two years. I was surprised that my father did not react like I expected him to. He had no problem with me quitting my job. He said, "You finished your studies and have proven yourself capable of good work, so you've achieved a lot already." He thought it would be good for me to see the world and that I would learn a lot from this experience.

It was harder for my mother to accept because she has such different beliefs and does not understand how I can travel around to promote the Bible, which she believes was just written by Jews to manipulate the world. But she changed her mind once she visited the ministry and saw that we offer the gospel only to those who are looking for the truth. We do not force anyone. She actually has become quite positive about it as she tells others about what I am doing.

My friends at work could not understand why I left to do missions. They were surprised that I was willing to do any kind of job that needed to be done, including cleaning toilets. They believe that when you have earned a degree, you deserve better jobs. Most of them would not be willing to do these minor jobs, but I have learned the benefits of serving with humility.

The best joke for them is the twenty dollars of spending money a month I am allowed (in addition to having all my housing, food, and medical needs taken care of). And of course they calculated how much money I needed to raise for support compared to what I could have earned during those two years—quite a financial loss! I believe that the fact that I left my job to be involved in missions made my coworkers think much more about my Christian beliefs than anything I ever said to them.

Bärbel started out struggling with what others would think of her desire to serve in missions. What would her father and mother say? How would her coworkers react? But she moved forward in faith and found God was faithful to either move in people's hearts to change them or to show her that obedience to Him is more important than what others think.

Going against the grain is actually a chance to be a witness to those who notice that you are doing something out of the ordinary. It is a way to show your faith in God, and His faithfulness to you as others observe you seeking His will, following His leading, making hard choices, and trusting Him to provide your support. Although we fear ridicule, I believe that when we live out our convictions and make personal sacrifices to serve others, we are just as likely to earn respect—maybe not at first but as we stick to what we know is right, like Mike and Bärbel did.

On the other hand, Jesus warned us that following Him means that people will react to us the way they reacted to Him. As His representatives, we can expect similar opposition to what He faced. Jesus warned in John 15:18–21:

If the world hates you, you know that it has hated Me

before it hated you. If you were of the world, the world would love its own; but because you are not of the world, but I chose you out of the world, because of this the world hates you. Remember the word that I said to you, 'A slave is not greater than his master.' If they persecuted Me, they will also persecute you; if they kept My word, they will keep yours also. But all these things they will do to you for My name's sake, because, they do not know the One who sent Me.

No matter how we live our lives, there may be people who disapprove, dislike, or even despise us. But whose approval matters the most? Are you willing to risk disobeying God's will to gain the approval of those whose standards or opinions do not line up with God's? Following God does not guarantee popularity or respect, but He does promise love, joy, and peace to those who yield to His Spirit. Obedience may cause a breach in some of our relationships, but our relationship with Him, and with those who love and serve Him along with us, often make up for our loss.

"God I offer You my pride that keeps me from reaching out to others."

"I have a fear of appearing foolish to the world. God, help me."

"Worrying too much about what people think of me. Being too anxious about my life. I need to trust in You more, Lord."

"I'm afraid of the reaction I'll get from the people I minister to. I pray to God that He helps me strengthen my faith so I may have total trust in Him."

"Lord, rid me of my pride. Help empty me of myself so I might encompass more of You."

"Give me freedom from the fear of disappointing other people, even those who love me and love God very much."

"Lord Jesus, I offer to You my desire to please people important to me. May I follow Your will alone. I offer to You my insecurities and inadequacies. Lord, may I find my identity in You."

"Lord, I offer You all of me that would hold back, all of my pride that will not let me share because of my fear of rejection, all of me that feels that I have to be perfect and cannot make mistakes."

"The fear of man brings a snare, but he who trusts in the LORD will be exalted" (Proverbs 29:25).

6

Personal Dreams, Agendas, Ambitions

Father, I offer you these things that might limit me from doing my part in seeing the nations worship you . . .

"My plans for life."

"My own agenda."

"North American/Asian Success Syndrome."

"A desire to have a name that others know and respect."

"Too many ambitions and dreams outside of God's will."

"My need to have a meaningful life."

"My own will that wants to excel in school/career for myself."

"Becoming caught in my hopes for my future, not listening to what You want in my future."

"Seeking my own glory."

"Conflicting views of my future between what I want and what God wants."

"Filial piety, personal success, financial security."

"My own personal ambition and plans that aren't in accordance with Yours."

The question, "What do you want to be when you grow up?" is something we hear a lot as children. As we progress in our education we are confronted with choices that ask us to have some idea of what we want to do in life. Parents, relatives, friends, teachers—all of them want to know what we see ourselves doing in the future, so we come up with a plan that sounds good to us. But sometimes God has a different plan, and asks us to be willing to change direction in obedience to Him.

Of course, this is not a new concept. God has been in the business of changing people's plans and vocations from the beginning. Moses went from being a prince to a shepherd to the leader of the nation of Israel. David was a shepherd boy who became a king. Some of the disciples started off as fishermen, and one was a tax collector. Saul never dreamed he would change from persecuting believers as an esteemed Jewish Pharisee to taking the gospel to the Gentiles as an apostle of Jesus Christ.

The exciting thing about God's plans is that they are custom made for us. Ephesians 2:10 tells us, "For we are His workmanship, created in Christ Jesus for good works, which God prepared beforehand so that we would walk in them." We were designed by Him with His purpose in mind, so when we follow His will for our lives we find it very fulfilling.

Kathi, from the United States, discovered that the Lord's plan for her was quite different from the career she and her family expected her to have. Now in retrospect she sees that the Lord designed her to be uniquely suited to the life He called her to.

I grew up in a medical family. My grandfather taught me, from the age of four, to tell people that I would be a doctor when I grew up. I went that route through school. I did very well in high school and my four years of university, majoring in biology as preparation for medical school. I gave my life to the Lord and accepted Him as my Savior when I turned sixteen. I just assumed He also wanted me to be a doctor.

At the end of my final year of university, after doing well in my medical school exams and interviews, the Lord revealed my heart to me. I was playing in a racquetball league. I really enjoyed it and was good at it. After a few months I began to feel a bit uncomfortable. I prayed and asked the Lord why. I remember kneeling beside my bed and the word *motive* kept coming to my mind. I decided to take a look, and a sick feeling came over me. I realized that winning in the league was important to me—more important than it should have been! It was feeding my ego and didn't seem right at the time. I decided to quit playing in the league, and an incredible sense of peace came over me.

The next day in my quiet time I was thanking the

Lord and praising Him. I felt Him ask me, "Kathi, do you remember when I asked you about your 'motive' in playing racquetball?" "Yes," I said. "The same is true about medical school." Again I felt a pit in my stomach. I had convinced myself that I wanted to go to medical school to help people. But when I asked myself the hard question about motive, I realized that I really wanted money and status. It was a shock to realize this. After a very short time of contemplation I withdrew my application to medical school knowing that I could never go for those reasons.

My family was not thrilled with my decision. My grandfather wanted to know if I had joined a cult and wondered if someone in my church had told me not to go to medical school. My parents, of course, wanted the best for me and wanted me to reach my best potential. I was honest with them about the struggles in my heart, and they supported me even though they didn't really understand.

My church was fantastic, and through its ministry I rededicated my life to the Lord. I earnestly sought His plan for my life and grew in character, love, and obedience. I became more involved: I joined a small group Bible study; began working at a Christian medical clinic, which was part of my church; and went through one-on-one discipleship with three different women for about two years each. I allowed them to ask me hard questions, learned much about the Father-heart of God, and began to trust Him more and more.

I was truly getting to the point where I wanted what God wanted. Many of my selfish ambitions were dying. A missionary came to our church and gave a presentation about what God was doing in the world. As I listened I felt not only the desire but also the freedom that I could pursue involvement in missions. After his presentation, as we were singing, I knew in my heart that this was God's best for me. My heart was burdened for Eastern Europe, which was also the prayer focus of our church. It was a confirmation for me when I spoke to the missionary after the service and he said that his organization was working in Eastern Europe (he hadn't mention that in his talk). I went on three summer outreaches and then joined full-time in 1989 to serve in Hungary.

I have *never* regretted not going to medical school. It is so clear to me that God created and prepared me to be a missionary, and I am very fulfilled. My biological father was quite an extrovert, and I inherited an adventurous spirit from him. I love new things and pioneering new ground, and living overseas has given me many opportunities for this. I love learning languages and have learned four new languages during my time in missions. I fit in and adapt easily. I have been trained in leadership, and I was the mission agency's country leader in Hungary for three years.

I am now married, and my husband is the leader of our team in South Africa. Because of my experience and gifting, I am able to partner effectively with him. I am responsible for senior leadership development on our team. I am also completing my master's degree in cultural anthropology. I train missionaries, who will serve in various countries, to deal with cultural issues. I love doing this and can only do it as a result of living in other cultures myself.

I am so grateful that the Lord redirected me from my own personal agenda to His. There is no greater joy or fulfillment than in doing His will.

Kathi has experienced what so many of us in missions have found—a deep sense of satisfaction and purpose in life, even in the midst of challenging circumstances. There is no greater peace or joy than being certain that you are in the place God wants you to be, doing what He wants you to do. But for most of us, finding that place is a process. We move toward a plan that makes sense to us, but if we are wise, we keep our hearts and minds open to being redirected by the Lord at any step along the way.

Keith, also from the United States, had his future all planned—a college degree in his career of choice, a job in that career, and plans to be married. Then he went on a short missions trip. He thought it was merely to give himself something to do during the school break, but God used it to change the course of his life.

I was attending a Bible college in southern California and finishing my senior year. That spring I was invited to go to Mexico with a mission group made up of young adults. I had nothing else to do for spring break, and no one wants to just stick around an empty campus, so I signed up. I thought a trip to Mexico sounded fun. It turned out to be an incredible eye-opener for me. I saw the way most of the world lives, and it touched my heart.

Back in school my thoughts drifted to the future. A job? A wife? I graduated and in that last week asked Rachael, my girlfriend, to marry me. That summer she went off to Spain for a short-term mission trip, and I headed to a camp where I had a summer position. My degree in college was in camp administration and recreation. Things looked very bright. I was doing what I loved, and soon I would be married. Rachael and I would start our lives together working in the ministry of Christian camping.

It all changed one evening sitting by myself out by the lake. I was having a quiet time with the Lord, and I was reading from Luke 14. Verses 26, 27, and 33 hit me hard:

> If anyone comes to Me, and does not hate his own father and mother and wife and children and brothers and sisters, yes, and even his own life, he cannot be My disciple. Whoever does not carry his own cross and come after Me cannot be My disciple. . . . So then, none of you can be My disciple who does not give up all his own possessions.

Basically the Holy Spirit challenged me right then and there. Unless I was willing to give up everything, I couldn't be His disciple. The truth of 100 percent commitment became so real. Was I willing to pick up my cross and be ready to die to follow Him? That night I got on my knees and said, "Lord, here I am; I want to follow You." If I had known at that time what it would cost me and where it would take me, I doubt I would have prayed those words. But God took me where I was. For me it meant a renewed effort to follow Jesus in my life.

Two days later I received a letter in the mail. It was from the mission group I had served with during spring break. Somehow because I had gone to Mexico during the spring break, they had my name on the list to join the one-year program. The letter was short and basically said that unless they heard from me they expected me in New Jersey at the end of the summer to go to Europe. My first reaction was "These guys are nuts!" But as I began to consider the timing of the letter in relationship to my fresh challenge of Luke 14, I thought maybe I should look into it. Maybe God was in this.

I couldn't let go of Luke 14, but I had some major obstacles in front of me: (1) no passport, (2) I had a contract with the camp to fulfill, (3) I had no money, and (4) I had just asked Rachael to marry me. So I took it to God in prayer. I simply said, "God if this is from You and You want me to do this, I will. But I have only three weeks to get a passport, raise support, get excused from my job, and see Rachael's mom to officially ask for her hand in marriage. If you can work out all these things, then I will go." I put a fleece before the Lord.

My boss at the camp was thrilled at the idea of me heading overseas for missions work! Not only would he let me go early from my contract but he also wanted to be the first one to support me for fifty dollars a month. He then helped me fill out the paper work to apply for my passport. For the return address I put the address of the mission agency's office in New Jersey, because they said it would take three to four weeks to get the passport. I had only three!

Then I contacted Rachael who was also supportive. She still had one year left at Bible college, so she would complete that while I was gone. So I headed off to Denver to meet up with Rachael and her mom, who gave her permission for our marriage. We then drove to see my folks in Washington State. We bought the engagement ring, and before I knew it I was on a plane to New Jersey. God had met every requirement. Along the way all the support I needed was raised. When I arrived in New Jersey they handed me my new passport—it had arrived the same day in the mail. We then drove over to New York to meet the others and fly off to Europe.

I will never forget how I felt sitting on that airplane. My favorite aunt summed it up wonderfully: she said I was completely out of my mind to run off and leave a wonderful girl like Rachael! A black depression settled in, and I sank lower and lower in my seat. I just kept saying, "What have I done? What have I done?"

During the orientation conference we needed to interview with different team leaders to see which ministry/country we would go to. I met an American named Norm who would lead the team that was going to Sudan. "Where is Sudan?" I wondered. The Sudan trip seemed like more of an adventure than all the others did. It would involve driving a truck from Germany down to Egypt and then up the Nile River to Sudan. But in my last interview with Norm, he looked me in the eye and asked me a very straightforward question, "Are you ready to die in Sudan?" I remember thinking, "What kind of a question is that? Look buddy, I'm here for one year, got it? I am engaged to a beautiful girl back home. I've got a life and a future waiting for me as soon as I finish this little excursion. When the year is up I'm out of here and back home. No one has asked me to die for anything before!" All these thoughts were rumbling through my mind. My only verbal response to him was

"Let me think about it."

I went away and thought and even prayed about it. I could not believe the gall of him asking me if I were willing to die in Sudan. I kept thinking that no one had ever asked me that before—but then it hit me pretty hard. Someone *had* asked me once before if I were willing to die. It was only a few weeks ago. It was Jesus. He had asked me that question while I sat by the shore of the lake. In that place, on my knees, I had told Him yes.

I went to Sudan. It was the most difficult purging time of my life. I came back broken. Rachael got a different fiancé back. But in my heart was placed a flame—a burning desire for the Muslim people that cannot be quenched. That was twenty-two years ago. The flame only burns hotter and deeper. Rachael and I never made it to a beautiful Christian camp in the Rockies, which had been my plan. Instead God has taken us to North Africa, the Middle East, and now, for the last ten years, the Arabian Peninsula. Here we have planted our feet in the sands of Arabia. Here, by His grace, we will stay until He releases us, or takes us home.

Both Keith and Kathi experienced the truth found in Proverbs 16:9. "The mind of man plans his way, But the LORD directs his steps." They were able to find God's plan for them because they asked for His leading and were willing to do whatever He would ask of them. God knows our hearts. When we are willing to submit to His will, He will direct us. Psalm 25:12 assures us saying, "Who is the man who fears the LORD? He will instruct him in the way he should choose."

Keith and Kathi both found that God had very different plans for their lives than the plans they had made for themselves. Neither

Keith nor Kathi regrets changing their plans in obedience to God's leading. Both say that God's plans have been very fulfilling—they wouldn't have wanted it any other way.

"Lord, I give you my ambitions, hopes, and dreams because I know You will not let me down. Forgive my fear and disbelief and pride."

"My plans—they keep me from You. please help me, God. I desire after Your plans."

"Lord, give me faith to follow. Help me to surrender my possessions, my desires, and my dreams. Let me be humble in the ministry that You'll put me in."

"My pride, independence, and ambitions—I lay them down here, Lord. Help me to stay strong and hold fast to this commitment."

"Pride, fear, worry, personal ambition—may whatever I do be for Your glory alone."

"God, this is a big step . . . but I can offer my ambitions and my pride and my desires to be comfortable above all. I also offer you the lies of my culture that have made me strive for wealth over You."

"Many plans are in a man's heart, But the counsel of the Lord will stand" (Proverbs 19:21).

7

Desire to Stay in My Comfort Zone

Father, I offer you these things that might limit me from doing my part in seeing the nations worship you . . .

"Lack of initiative, being self-conscious, being in a rut, being comfortable, my desire for financial success, lack of will."

"Desire for personal wealth."

"My fear of leaving all I have and serving you! But I will with your strength."

"Fear of being taken out of my comfort zone that I have built up for a long time—and my selfishness and pride."

"I want a comfortable life and fear suffering."

"Distractions and 'stuff'"

"Fear of leaving my comfort zone."

"The sacrifice."

"Financially comfortable future."

"1: My pile of stuff.
2: Eyeritis [Iritis].
3: An overly fast, overly full lifestyle.
4: Comfort."

"Fear, laziness, and being too comfortable in my North American life."

Over a quarter of the students' responses on the Wall involved some kind of desire to have a comfortable life, material possessions, control over their own lives—basically a desire to remain in their comfort zone. Unfortunately, being raised in affluence, materialism, and a lot of personal freedom leads us to believe that we need much more than we do. It is difficult for us to imagine giving all that up, especially since we are exposed to the constant barrage of advertisements that tells us our happiness depends on it.

But when we trust God to take care of our needs, we learn several things. One is that things do not bring us happiness, but a life lived in obedience and dependence on God provides happiness, peace, and joy. Another is that we do not need as much as we thought we did to get along quite well. Also, we are usually surprised by how much God actually does provide for us—more than we expected—in ways that show His loving care and knowledge of our needs and desires. If He does not provide it, we do not really need it. But if we do need it, He provides it at just the right time, often teaching us some kind of lesson in the process.

Our comfort zone is not just limited to material comforts like food, clothing, or a nice place to live. Things like relationships, cultural differences, expectations (ours and others), and fears of various sorts also affect our comfort. Stacy, from the United States, let her desire for many of these things, and fear of others, keep her from obeying God's call for many years.

I first felt the call to mission work many years ago as a single person. I attended mission conferences at church and sensed a pull to be willing to go overseas. I never wanted to leave my comfort zone, was greatly afraid to, but still sensed that pull.

Later, when I married Chuck, I knew there was a strong likelihood that we would go overseas, because he had been to Yugoslavia, had loved it there, and wanted to go back. I knew I did not want to go there, or anywhere else, but knew I was opening the door to this possibility by marrying him.

After four years of marriage, I agreed to go on a four-week summer program to Germany, which ended with a mission experience in the housing projects of inner-city Dublin. I sensed that we both fit in well and had a strong desire to go back. We started working toward that end, but I still did not want to go. My main obstacle then was thinking I would have to attend Bible school.

I also really wanted children, and we were in the process of beginning a domestic adoption, which is a long, involved process. I also knew that neither of our families would want us to go, as neither were believers nor would they want their first grandchild to be out of the country. I basically got cold feet about going overseas, and we stopped the process.

What was I afraid of? Many things: that I wouldn't be able to handle it, that I'd "go nuts," and that I wouldn't be able to adopt a second child.

We waited, due to my fears and desires, for another seven years. One Christmas I read an article on faith in *Discipleship Journal* that Sue Kline, a friend of mine, had written. She asked the question, "What are the biggest things we fear, or lack faith in?" I knew right away that mine had to do with mission work. I made the decision then and there that I would take the next step. I was not ready to jump fully into the work but was willing to work toward it. God honored that small step of obedience.

About that time my husband told me about a Perspectives course that would be starting soon. I had heard about this course for years, how good and life-changing it was. It was a long course, which meant a big commitment, and I always felt I had neither the time nor the desire to go. This time I had the desire to make the time. It had now become very important to me.

I had decided to go on a short-term trip with my husband to see how we would do together (really to see how I would do overseas). When I went to the Perspectives course I heard about a trip to Kazakhstan. I had never even heard of that country, but the more I heard about it and that particular trip, the more I sensed that God was leading us there. The outreach involved building relationships and music, which interested us. As we pursued this I quickly became convinced that God wanted us to go and that He would get us there, even though we only had a very short time to raise funds.

Oddly enough, Chuck thought we should wait a year to prepare and go the next summer. We had totally switched sides! Here, after so many years of wanting to go overseas, Chuck did not believe it could happen. But it did; we were able to raise the funds in time and we went.

Once we got to Kazakhstan, I loved the people and was touched by the warm hospitality they showed, even to total strangers. However, I was also greatly depressed by the physical appearance of the city—old, brown, ugly, decaying former-Soviet buildings with dirt and trash everywhere. I kept thinking, "Why don't they spend some money to repair things and clean them up?" Even then, I knew we would be returning there to live, but I did not want to. I began to cry.

Chuck had hit it off with the professor of physics at a local university and was asked to return as a lecturer in physics. (Chuck had a degree in aerospace engineering and had a good job.) I felt comfortable with that idea. It meant that Chuck could take a sabbatical from work and we would be gone for a set time. We would return to a job with security and, best of all, not have to raise support. For some reason I did not mind raising support for a short trip but was uncomfortable about asking people for money long term. I basically told God that I would go to Kazakhstan on the stipulation that Chuck could get this sabbatical.

He couldn't; it didn't work out. There was a new director of the university, so all the politics and relationships connected with Chuck's invitation changed. Suddenly both Chuck and I felt like we did not know what else we would do with our lives if we did not go overseas. Emotionally, we were both at the point of expecting to go overseas, and if we were not doing that, then what?

Finally, Chuck wrestled with God and made the life-changing decision that, yes, we would go overseas, even if we had to raise support. I agreed. Wait—did I just say that? I couldn't believe it myself! I had come full circle on the issue, and I knew this was one more obstacle the Lord wanted me to trust Him with.

Then there was the issue of our parents. Neither of our parents were believers nor were the rest of our immediate families. We had two boys and the only grandchildren on either side. We knew both sets of parents would be against our going—but God worked even that out. Even though our parents did not really want us to go overseas, they did not make a big fuss. They were as supportive as they could be, even though they would miss the boys and us greatly and worry a lot to boot.

Stacy had tried to avoid many types of uncomfortable situations over the years—tension and disapproval from parents; raising support; living in poor, ugly conditions; uncertainty about adoptions—basically she was unwilling to give up her desires and comfort to follow what she knew God wanted. But God persistently worked in her heart and through her circumstances to bring her and her husband to the place where He wanted them—desiring His will over their own comfort. They discovered the truth of Psalm 37:4: "Delight yourself in the LORD and He will give you the desires of your heart." No, not that He will give you everything you want, but as you delight yourself in Him, He will place His desires in your heart. Your desires start matching up with what He desires for you, and then He freely fulfills those desires. Stacy's desire to go only under certain circumstances (that is, a paying job for her husband with a time limit) was eventually changed to a desire to go, even if they had to raise support and face family disapproval. God fulfilled those desires by providing their support and minimizing their parents' resistance.

The apostle Paul found himself in a variety of circumstances throughout his ministry, including a lot of time in prison. Here is his perspective on the issue:

Not that I speak from want, for I have learned to be content in whatever circumstances I am. I know how to get along with humble means, and I also know how to live in prosperity; in any and every circumstance I have learned the secret of being filled and going hungry, both of having abundance and suffering need. I can do all things through Him who strengthens me. (Philippians 4:11–13)

Jan, from the United States, learned this same lesson and gives us some insight into what it is like to give up an American lifestyle to live in another culture.

Moving to Colombia as a missionary certainly moved me out of my comfort zone. I will never forget being on that plane to Costa Rica for our year of language study thinking, "I must be crazy to take two babies, bottles, and all of our stuff and leave the country I know and love for the rest of my life." But my husband's calling was to Colombia, which meant I was also called there, so I trusted the Lord above and beyond those immediate circumstances.

That first year was especially challenging with the inconvenience of taking two babies to a foreign country where I would be in language school. God gave me the physical and emotional ability to do that, because these are not the comfortable things in life. Another challenge was living in constant upset until we were finally able to put down roots. After arriving in Colombia we were able to rent a house after looking, on foot and by taxi, for a couple of weeks. It came with a dining room table and twelve chairs. Other than that we had nothing and had to begin to get things together, starting with mattresses. Our sparsely furnished apartment made me think of the beautiful couch I had just sold in the States. You soon learn that materialism is not important when you find you can live with very little.

My husband, Howard, had grown up in Colombia, so I had the peculiar challenge of fitting into his home culture and what was comfortable for him. First, there was the language issue. He had grown up with Spanish and was totally bilingual. I was just learning. He already knew the culture and the people. It was like coming home for him. I knew no one and started from scratch.

The differences between our two countries did not faze him, but I had to deal with each one on a daily basis. Colombia is Third World, so I missed the many conveniences I was used to. The food was different.

Shopping was different. Cooking was different. It was nice having a maid, but this was new to me, and I did not know quite what to do or how that operated. Church was in Spanish, and there was no nursery in those days. We went to church by taking two busses, carrying two children plus Bibles, hymnals, and a diaper bag.

The first two years were a challenge. One of the first lessons I had to learn was to rest in God, to go at His pace, and to realize that people were not dying to see me or hear my message of hope and salvation. Many times we missionaries are led to believe that there will be people on our doorsteps just waiting to hear the gospel. Nothing was further from the truth. I had to earn my right to be in their country. I had to make friends. I had to learn to love them. I had to show that love—this was all a process.

Often God needs to first teach us some important lessons. Getting us out of our comfort zone allows Him to teach us things we otherwise might never learn.

It is always hard to leave family and friends behind, but the Lord gives you new ones, not right away, but He does; and today we have a congregation of 1,500 people whom we love and who seem very much like family and certainly close friends.

There is that leap of faith in all of this and the inevitable time periods where you wonder where it is all heading—but I will say that of our thirty-three years here, thirty-one of them have been comfortable! So the first two years had to occur in order to experience what we have since.

Jan learned that God is faithful to supply what she needs. Jesus Himself assures us of this truth in Matthew 6:25–26, 31–33:

For this reason I say to you, do not be worried about your life, as to what you will eat or what you will drink; nor for your body, as to what you will put on. Is not life more than food, and the body more than clothing? Look at the birds of the air, that they do not sow, nor reap nor gather into barns, and yet your heavenly Father feeds them. Are you not worth much more than they? . . . Do not worry then, saying, 'What will we eat?' or 'What will we drink?' or 'What will we wear for clothing?' For the Gentiles eagerly seek all these things; for your heavenly Father knows that you need all these things. But seek first His kingdom and His righteousness, and all these things will be added to you.

Sometimes the issue is not worrying about the future but just becoming comfortable with your situation and having expectations that get in the way of what God has called you to do. Rick, from the United States, found himself being wooed from his intentions of serving in missions to pursuing the typical American dream.

I was stretching out my seminary studies a bit, partly for financial reasons. I was studying part-time and working at UPS part-time. It was getting close to graduation time, and I was not really making any specific plans. I was getting too settled with a local church full of seminary students and ex-students, all looking for answers. Although there was quite an emphasis on discovering your gifts, friendship evangelism, and power evangelism, the mission vision seemed to be very dim—

even though a number of us were in the seminary for cultural or missions studies.

I also had a girlfriend and a job that could lead to your typical white-picket-fence American existence. I was thinking that within a year I could actually move up in the UPS system, but then suddenly it was wake-up time. "Hey, what am I doing with my original desire to go somewhere in the world for the Lord?" I wondered. "Isn't that why I came to this seminary?" Coincidentally, some mission representatives were on campus, and I found that I could use my mime skills on a team in Belgium. I decided to join them for one year, but I have stayed for fifteen!

Rick came close to accepting the world's value system instead of following what he had believed was God's direction for his life. It was subtle, but it threatened to sidetrack him. Perhaps Romans 12:1–2 helped to get him back on track:

Therefore I urge you, brethren, by the mercies of God, to present your bodies a living and holy sacrifice, acceptable to God, which is your spiritual service of worship. And do not be conformed to this world, but be transformed by the renewing of your mind, so that you may prove what the will of God is, that which is good and acceptable and perfect.

"I offer my comfy, suburban lifestyle, Jesus."

"Please pray for my willingness to go out of my comfort zone to put my trust in the Lord over my finances, relationships, and family—and to go out for His great command!"

"Lord, I give You these things: my fear of being oppressed, myself, my desire to live comfortably, and my pride. Please forgive me for hindering the work You want to do in me."

"I offer You my own self-seeking, worldly desires for my future that would hold me back from your call."

"My Lord, I give You my comforts, expectations, fears, and dreams. May You be glorified."

"Lord, take my life and make it fully Your own. Take my spoiled American attitude and grace it with Your pure and sacrificial love. Thank You, Lord, for sparing me the horrors of life that many face daily. Please give me wisdom and grace, compassion and love, commitment and peace to truly make a difference to many—that they may know Your heartfelt love and experience freedom, joy, and peace ever in You. Amen."

"But godliness actually is a means of great gain when accompanied by contentment. For we have brought nothing into the world, so we cannot take anything out of it either. If we have food and covering, with these we shall be content. But those who want to get rich fall into temptation and a snare and many foolish and harmful desires which plunge men into ruin and destruction. For the love of money is a root of all sorts of evil, and some by longing for it have wandered away from the faith and pierced themselves with many griefs. But flee from these things, you man of God, and pursue righteousness, godliness, faith, love, perseverance and gentleness" (1 Timothy 6:6–11).

8

Parental Disapproval

$\mathbf{F}$ather, I offer you these things that might limit me from doing my part in seeing the nations worship you . . .

"Family opinion of what I should do with my life."

"My fears in needing to please my parents."

"Discouragement from non-Christian parents."

"Fears and family pressures."

"My comfortable future, my education, my parents (whom I love so much)—I am afraid of disappointing my parents."

"The priorities of the world, and the dreams of my parents, as well as my own dreams."

"Fear of change. Fear of what my dad will say."

"Fear of not pleasing my non-believing dad."

"My parents' pressure to keep my career."

Over 20 percent of the responses on the Wall had to do with relationships. Of those, about a third mentioned their parents' response as an obstacle they faced. The good news is that these students care what their parents think. The bad news is that their parents seem to be opposed to the idea of them serving in missions, at least that is what they think. Can God overcome this obstacle?

Christy, an American now working in the United Kingdom, struggled with a conflict between her desire to serve in missions, which she believed was God's will for her life, and obeying her parents, who were opposed to her plans. There seemed to be Scriptures on both sides of the issue. How could she reconcile them and know what to do?

"Children obey your parents in the Lord, for this is right. Honor your father and mother (which is the first commandment with a promise), that it may be well with you, and that you may live long on the earth" (Ephesians 6:1–3).

I knew this Scripture and understood what God was asking me to do, but did He really understand my situation? What about when I feel that what He wants me to do is against my parents' desires?

During one year at university I was trying to plan my summer. I had mentioned to my parents that I was considering serving as a summer missionary but did not know where. They encouraged me and said that I should do whatever I wanted. I looked at my options and was ecstatic when I felt that the Lord was asking me to go to East Asia. I thought I had discovered the perfect way to spend my summer. It was a five-week assignment working in an East Asian camp teaching English to young students. It was exactly what I enjoyed doing and who I wanted to serve.

I made a phone call home to discuss the details with my parents and was stunned to find that they did not approve. I was heartbroken. I could not understand why just a few weeks before they had told me I could do whatever I wanted, and now they were changing their minds! I felt hurt, angry, disappointed, frustrated, and betrayed.

I asked God what He was doing in this situation. Why would He call me somewhere if I could not go? Why did I have to decide between my parents and the Lord's work? I felt a hunger to share the gospel with these people that I had never met but also a deep desire to honor and obey my parents, as God commands. How could both things—both from God—be in such conflict with one another? I prayed that He would change my parents' hearts, or change mine in the process.

As I continued to seek God about this decision I began to discover more in the Bible that challenged me. The Ten Commandments, Ephesians 6:1–2, Colossians 3:20, Romans 1:30, 2 Timothy 3:2, and other verses teach about children honoring their parents.

For days I wrestled with what to do. I cried as I prayed for God's wisdom. My emotions were raging inside of me. As I examined the Scriptures, I knew what God was asking me to do—He wanted me to obey my parents' desires. God was showing me several truths.

- God wants me to honor my mother and father. This was His command, and I was to obey (Psalm 119:1–6). The Scriptures warn us about having a rebellious heart (1 Samuel 12:15).
- God can use my parents even though my dad is not a follower of Christ. God is in control. If He really wants me to go, God has the ability to change my dad's heart. I need to trust in God's sovereignty (Psalm 84:12).
- God wants me to humble myself and submit, because I do not know where my dad stands with Christ. Going against his will would hinder future communication and ruin my witness to him (2 Corinthians 6:3).
- God wants me to lay down all of my desires, surrendering control of everything, so that He can work through them. Even if I think my desires are from Him, if I give them to God, He will bless me (Psalm 27:13–14).

Many questioned my reasoning and wondered how I could obey an unbelieving father. They quoted Matthew 10:35–37, "For I came to set a man against his father, and a daughter against her mother, and a daughter-in-law against her mother-in-law, and a man's enemies will be the members of his household."

I was confused by this passage. Why would God tell us to honor our parents but then turn from them later? I again turned to the Lord in prayer, and He opened my eyes to the Scriptures that follow:

He who loves father or mother more than Me is not worthy of Me; and he who loves son or daughter more than Me is not worthy of Me. And he who does not take his cross and follow after Me is not worthy of Me. He who has found his life shall lose it, and he who has lost his life for My sake shall find it. (Matthew 10:37–39)

This passage confirmed what I'd already felt God telling me. I realized two important things from this passage:

- Division occurs for the cause of Christ. Others may ask me to do things that are against God, but I need to stand firm and be ready to face opposition, even from my parents.
- Division occurs when you love others, including your family, more than God. Jesus tells us the most important thing is that He is first in our lives.

I realized my parents were not asking me to do something that was against God. They were not asking me to denounce God and turn away from Christianity. Instead, they were asking me to find another way to serve Him.

My greatest wish is to serve God in full-time ministry, and I was hoping that my parents would give in at any moment. God would not tell me to obey my parents and then ask me to disobey.

I told God I could not go without both of my parents'

permission and blessing. I was firm in my convictions, and knew I had made a choice that pleased God. I went to my parents with humility and told them my decision. They were grateful, and I could see my decision gained me their respect.

As I began to submit to my parents in other ways, I began to see my dad's heart becoming softer. As I trusted God to work in me and through me, my dad and I became closer and he could see visible changes in me.

During my last year at university I began to look for a job. God led me to a full-time position in the United Kingdom as a missionary. I immediately realized that the job and location were perfect for me. I knew God was calling me to serve Him in this position—I just needed the approval of my parents.

When I found the opportunity in the U.K., I sent them a copy of the job description. I nervously waited and prayed for God's providence in the situation. My mother said she was excited because I had found a job that is perfectly suited for me. She and my dad were both thrilled and knew that this is where I should be. I thanked God for His ability to work things out for my good and His glory.

As I began the application process, I started seeing God's wisdom and control of the situation. My parents began to ask questions and wanted to be a part of what I was doing. They guided me through the application process and encouraged me. They helped me during the long packing process and stood beside me during the tough goodbyes.

I'm now a missionary serving for two years in the United Kingdom. I stand in awe of the ways God has honored my obedience to His Word. Because of my submission He has richly blessed my parents, my ministry, and me. It was not easy, but I know it is one of the best decisions I have made. Because I said, "I can't go," I have, through God's strength and grace, been able to:

- Share the gospel with my dad.
- Gain the respect of my dad and have him listen to me.
- Have my parents be a part of what I am now doing.
- Grow closer in my relationship with my parents.
- Receive the blessing of God in my ministry and life.

At the time I did not understand why I was giving up my desire—God never showed or promised me anything. It is only now, four years later, that I am beginning to see how God has provided. I am a missionary—something I never thought possible two years ago.

I know I will never truly understand the impact of my decision, especially concerning my father. The respect my father has for me because I have honored him has opened up more doors to communicate with him. When I think about where I might be right now if I had said yes two years ago, I'm grieved. My parents would have cut me off, and I would be without my parents' support. The opportunities to tell my dad about the Lord would have never existed.

Christy felt the Lord directing her to wait and trust the Lord to change her parents' hearts. It took a few years, but God used that time to refine her, redirect her, and work in her relationship with her parents. She recognized the authority of her parents at this stage of her life and realized that God could use that to guide her. She submitted to them, trusting God to direct her through them, even though her father was not a believer.

Ben, an American, found himself in a different situation. He was not under the authority of his father and stepmother but faced a decision that would greatly affect his relationship with them.

I was born in 1951 in a home with a driven, absentee father married to his work. Soon my parents' marriage broke up, my older sister and I were awarded to my mom by the courts, and we moved to California from the East Coast. After a short period of time my mom suffered health problems, and we went to live with my father and stepmother for two years. We returned to live with my mom after she recovered.

At this time all ties were broken with my real father and stepmother until I found them twelve years later. The next ten years were okay until my new stepfather felt, for various reasons, that he could not cope with life. He committed suicide by leaping into the Pacific Ocean. This happened in 1969 just after I had attended a Young Life summer camp in northern California and committed myself to follow the Lord.

Being in high school and an avid long distance runner, I tried to hide from the pain of his death through running. My walk with God was put on hold while I struggled with the concept of God being a God of love. I went on to college and during my first year placed seventeenth in all of southern California in cross-country running. But God was not through with me yet. A short time later I suffered a serious injury to my arch, which ended my running career and started me on a new journey. This journey eventually led me into full-time missionary service.

After my second year of college I took a number of trips in an old VW Bus. On one of these trips I discovered the location of my real father and stepmother. As I was making my way to visit them, I encountered a group of Christian guys who had a tremendous influence on me and helped me rededicate my life to Christ. I had a new desire to grow in my walk and to serve Him.

One week later I drove up to the townhouse in Maryland where my father and stepmother lived. They were happy to see me but not happy about my commitment to the Lord. Later that summer I returned to California to attend the University of California, Santa Cruz. I was discipled over the next two years by an InterVarsity student group. I dedicated myself to becoming a cross-cultural witness through my contact with an evangelist named Ken. After graduation I requested to go to Israel with a student exchange program, but there were some obstacles to overcome.

After the death of my stepfather my mother remained a widow, so I felt responsible to take care of her. As I talked with her, she assured me in no uncertain terms that she was giving her blessing to my goal to go to Israel, even though she did not share my newfound faith. She had my sister to help her and she wanted me to be free to go after my dream.

On my way to Israel, en route to my transcontinental flight to Tel Aviv, I was able to stop over on the East Coast so I could say goodbye to my father and stepmother. They had me over for dinner, and it was then that my stepmother said quite calmly, "If you become a full-time Christian worker, you will no longer be considered our son." I wondered about this comment, since I was not going to Israel to become involved in full-time Christian ministry—or so I thought.

In the fall of the first year I was in Israel I came in contact with a particular mission group. I worked with their teams part-time while living on a kibbutz in northern Israel. The next spring God began speaking to me about going full-time with this group. I remembered my parents' warning that going into full-time Christian work would mean that I would be disowned from any inheritance and might end my newfound relationship with them. I really struggled between recognizing and following the Lordship of Christ in my life and possibly losing, once again, the connection with my father. In the end I laid my relationship with my father on the altar of God and surrendered my future to the Lord. An overwhelming peace went through my whole being.

The letters I wrote to my father and stepmother about my plans to become a missionary were not answered; however, I would contact them whenever I was in the States and was still welcome to visit them. In 1983, after eight years, my father said, "I am happy that you are my son." This was a real breakthrough for me, and over the years I stayed in touch with them by phone. In 1998 I again visited my father and stepmother. My father and I had the best time together. My stepmother died soon after that, and my father went to live with my brother until he died two years later without showing much interest in spiritual things. The time together in 1998 was a real highlight of my life, to be able to just love my dad and stepmom.

At the reading of my father's will I heard that I had been denied any of the inheritance I should have received. This hurt me, and yet I look back at the last two and half decades and can see many blessings. The last twenty-six years have seen my mom well taken care of by my sister. She is happy and over the last twenty years has come to a growing and deepening faith.

Through the events of a twice broken home, I came into full-time Christian work fearing failure in ministry and marriage. Since leaving the States in 1975 God has been faithful in both areas in spite of my fears. The ministry has been blessed with many opportunities to witness in several foreign countries, and my wife and I have just celebrated our fifteenth anniversary of a growing and deepening marriage.

I have experienced the truth of Jesus' words in Matthew 19:29: "And everyone who has left houses or brothers or sisters or father or mother or children or farms for My name's sake, will receive many times as much, and will inherit eternal life."

Christy and Ben found themselves in different situations as they faced parental disapproval. Each asked the Lord for insight and guidance and each received direction specific to His will for them. Eventually, the Lord brought the parents into an acceptance of their son's or daughter's desire to serve in missions—but, in Ben's case, not until he had counted the cost and decided to follow the Lord's calling in spite of the possibility of losing the relationship with his parents.

God asks us to put Him first and obey Him above all others.

He is also capable of changing the hardest of hearts, and He wants us to trust Him to work as we honor our parents. Sometimes He expects us to follow His lead in spite of the response of our family.

How we go about the process can make a big difference. Even if we feel we must go against our parents' wishes in order to obey the Lord, we must still show respect to our parents. Our attitude can make a huge difference. If you come across as rebellious with an "I don't care what you think; I have to obey God, and you are standing in my way" attitude you can do great damage to your relationship and witness to your parents.

Many verses in Proverbs encourage us to listen to our parents' advice, and we are wise to talk through the issues with them. We may find that the things that concern them about our desire to serve in missions are not what we expect. They might have valid concerns that need to be considered. God often uses our parents to guide or redirect us like He did in Christy's story.

Sometimes our desire to serve God in another country can feel like rejection to the family left behind. Talking things through with them and taking them with you through the process of discovering God's will and finding the right mission opportunity may help them see that this is the right thing for you.

But then sometimes your faith and values are so different from your parents' that you will feel you must respectfully disagree with their desires in order to follow God's clear will for your life, like Ben did.

How this all works out in each of our lives will vary, requiring us to seek His guidance, listen closely for His direction, allow Him to work in us and our parents, and respond as He leads.

James 1:5 can encourage us: "But if any of you lacks wisdom, let him ask of God, who gives to all men generously and without reproach, and it will be given to him." God wants us to know His will. If we are committed to doing His will, He will show us what He wants us to do.

"Lord, I offer up to You my fears of what it means to obey You. Financial problems as well. Lastly, I lift up to You my parents. May they object to my passion to missions only in accordance with Your will."

"My materialism, my desire to be beautiful, my fear of disappointing my parents—O God, take them!"

"Responsibility to my parents and the gifts they have given me. May their hopes come to meld with Yours, Father."

"The fear that I will be cut off, rejected, and etc. by my family; and yet I know that I have a Heavenly Father in whom I trust. I must follow Him until the end of my days, no matter where He leads me. Here I am, Lord, send me."

"My son, obey your father's commands, and don't neglect your mother's teaching. Keep their words always in your heart. Tie them around your neck. Wherever you walk, their counsel can lead you. When you sleep, they will protect you. When you wake up in the morning, they will advise you. For these commands and this teaching are a lamp to light the way ahead of you. The correction of discipline is the way to life" (Proverb 6:20–23, NLT).

"If you want to be my follower you must love me more than your own father and mother, wife and children, brothers and sisters—yes, more than your own life. Otherwise, you cannot be my disciple" (Luke 14:26, NLT).

9

Personal Relationships: Present and Future

Father, I offer you these things that might limit me from doing my part in seeing the nations worship you . . .

"My desire for human relationships to fulfill needs that only You can."

"My yearning for human love."

"Fear, loneliness, being away from family and friends."

"For His glory I need to let guys go."

"My post-high school future and my boyfriend/future mate worries."

"My desire to have a boyfriend and get married soon."

"My desire to have marriage now and not wait to trust that You know what's best for me."

"My atheist boyfriend."

"Fear of not having a companion on the field and being way too picky."

"Looking for God's will and direction with a new baby coming and finding what He wants to do with us as we start a family."

"Fear of going alone."

"I am scared to be without friends and family—I would be alone."

"Putting love of people ahead of God."

"Fear of change—leaving the community I already have."

"Insecurities and over-dependence on relationships."

Many of the responses on the wall involved concerns about relationships. Some were about current relationships, like leaving behind family and friends, or giving up a romantic relationship with someone who is not interested in missions. Some had to do with the fear of being lonely on the mission field. Many had concerns about finding a husband or wife and someday having a family.

We have been created as social beings who need personal

relationships, so these are natural, God-given desires. Our desires are not wrong unless they get in the way of what the Lord wants us to do. When fulfilling our desires becomes more important than obeying God, that becomes a problem. God asks us to seek and do His will first, and if we do, He promises to take care of our needs (Matthew 6).

Psalm 37:4 says, "Delight yourself in the LORD; And He will give you the desires of your heart." The key to this promise is delighting in the Lord. As we choose to be content and happy with what He provides and where He leads, our desires line up with His desires for us. If He desires that we remain single, He can give us contentment and peace with that if we let Him. He can provide close friends and "family" to meet our needs for relationships anywhere He leads us. And He fulfills our desire for a spouse, when it matches His plan for us, at the right time and with the right person.

Barb is an American who was afraid that going into the mission field single would mean remaining single. She had to come to a place where she was willing to trust the Lord to either remove her desire to get married or fulfill it in His own timing. Once she gave her desire over to Him, she found Him to be faithful.

I was in Korea with a singing group on a short-term assignment when I felt the Lord calling me to long-term service there. I was willing and excited to go, except for one obstacle. I was afraid that I would not meet anyone I could marry and that I would remain single if I stayed overseas for any length of time.

I wrestled with this issue and finally read a book that I had known about but had been avoiding—*Single and Satisfied*. I was not sure I wanted to be satisfied with being single! But reading it did the trick. I became convinced that if God wanted me to be single He would be all that I needed and I would be satisfied. On the other hand, if God did have a man in my plan then He would bring about our meeting and I didn't need to worry about it. I figured that the latter was highly unlikely given where I would be serving, so I surrendered to Him my desire to marry, which had been strong since I was a young girl. I would go, even if it meant remaining single.

Three weeks after that I met a young, single missionary named Jerry at a planning meeting for a high school outreach. This event would feature our singing group in a camp setting, and he was on the camp board. He was twenty-nine and had been serving in Korea for a number of years. He was fairly sure the Lord was also asking him to be single, though his real heart's desire was to be married. When we met we discovered our mutual love for the Lord and call to serve in Korea. We immediately were interested in each other and recognized that God had brought us together. We found that as we were each following God's plan individually, His plan for us to serve together in Korea as a married couple came together.

Barb and Jerry's story reminds me of some advice I once heard someone give to young singles who were wondering how to go about finding a husband or wife. She said, "Run as fast as you can in the direction that the Lord is leading you, keeping your eyes on Him. As you run, if you notice someone running beside you in the same direction, take a good look. That just might be God's choice of a partner for you."

Some couples, like Barb and Jerry, have found each other on

their way to obeying God's call. Many missionary couples have found each other as they were serving in the place the Lord directed them to.

Mark is an American who had already been serving as a missionary in the Arab world for several years when he met the young woman he wanted to marry. But there were some tricky obstacles to overcome in the areas of geography and finance.

I was thirty-four years old, single, and interested in getting married. I had met a nice woman at the conference that my mission organization holds each year. Missionaries from all over the world attend this conference, so it is a great place to meet women who are already called to missions, especially for single men living in the Arab world. As our relationship developed I started thinking about the future and what would be involved if we wanted to pursue a future together.

I had a lot of financial concerns about getting married. My support level was adequate for a single person, but I did not have the money to provide for a wife, much less a family. How would I buy an engagement and wedding ring, and how could I possibly afford a honeymoon aside from camping? Would she be interested in coming to the Arab world and living amongst Muslims? Having been in North Africa for seven years, I was out of touch with dating, much less asking a woman to marry me! But the ability to provide financially for my wife was the biggest fear. I could offer so little since I did not own a house, a car, or much of anything else. What woman in her right mind would marry me? Whose father would let his daughter marry me?

I sought counsel from various leaders in my mission

organization, and the final conclusion was that I was simply going to have to trust God that He would provide. It was a big step of faith for me, since a man wants to be able to provide for his new bride. After much prayer I asked this woman to leave the Eastern European country where she was serving and return to the United States so we could spend some time together and see if this was really what the Lord wanted for us.

Soon after my arrival back home, and with plans to marry, God began to work through His people in amazing ways. First, one of my supporters called me and said that she had an old ring, which had belonged to an aunt. It contained five diamonds, and she would like to give it to me! I took the ring and had the diamonds removed and reset into an engagement ring and earrings. When I went to the jewelry store to pick up the ring and earrings, the owner told me that the bill had been paid. I could hardly believe it! An old friend of mine had paid the bill.

We were engaged and immediately started to make wedding plans. We had a simple wedding in a log cabin church followed by a beautiful reception in the church basement. For our honeymoon the aunt of my new wife offered us her lake house in the mountains for two weeks at no charge. We had an awesome honeymoon—just twenty minutes from the church.

Someone provided us with a car, which we donated to our church when we returned to the mission field for the use of missionaries coming home on furlough.

My wife has now joined me in living in the Arab world and is reaching out to Muslims. We have one child with another on the way, and God continues to provide for all our needs. It is amazing how He moves in the hearts of His people to give. It has not only strengthened my faith but also encouraged me to be a better giver to others.

Of course, the best gifts He has provided for me are my lovely wife and children. He is the giver of good things to His people and delights in meeting not only our needs but, often, even our desires.

We have a creative God, who works in surprising ways to meet our needs, even when we cannot figure out how it will happen. Mark saw God providing for him in ways he could not foresee, through people he never would have expected (and some he did not yet know.) Part of the fun and blessing of serving God is seeing how He provides.

Our need for relationships is not limited to marriage partners only. We need people in our lives to accept us, love us, encourage us, challenge us, confront us, hold us accountable, and play with us. When we are away from home, we need people to become our family. How wonderful that believers are called "the family of God"—brothers and sisters in Christ. There is a real bond between believers that overcomes cultural and language barriers. Part of the blessing of being a missionary is experiencing the extended family of God all over the world.

Gary, an American who is serving in a large community of missionaries, found himself missing his family even though he was surrounded by people. Sometimes loneliness is more a state of mind, but the Lord helped Gary to see that He had provided for him in a special way.

I was sitting at breakfast all by myself, because the table with my friends was full of other people. I figured that if I were all by myself at a table that seats eight surely someone would join me. It was my birthday, and I wanted to share it with someone. At home at least someone would take notice and wish me a happy birthday. As adults we tell ourselves that it really doesn't matter. What is another birthday? But as I sat and ate my whole breakfast, all alone, I felt homesick and wished my family were with me. I started feeling sorry for myself. (Not a good thing to do!)

I went to work, and the boss gave out the work assignments. I started with a "woe is me" attitude. On my way to fix an electrical problem, someone said, "Hi Gary. Happy birthday." Then two more people said the same thing. Now in a community of over 300 people, how did they know it was my birthday? Before lunch time at least twenty-five more people said, "Happy birthday." Some even told me that they had prayed for me that morning.

One couple asked me if I would have dinner with them that night. That was no problem, since we all have dinner together in the dining room anyway. I grabbed a tray and some food and went to the table. Soon they joined me with a homemade cake, plates, and a knife. The woman had gone to the expense and trouble of making a birthday cake for me! I had dinner with my wonderful friends. I do not remember what we had for dinner, but I do remember the love and friendship.

As we were eating I heard some loud humming, and fifty or sixty people gathered around the table. The humming turned into, "Happy birthday to you. HEY! Happy birthday to you. HEY! Happy birthday to Gary..." (rumble and shouting and clapping for fifteen seconds), "Happy birthday to you!" (more applause). I think it was the best birthday I'd had in years!

Gary's birthday provided an opportunity for God to give him a gift—the realization that He had surrounded him with friends and "family" who cared for him in the absence of his real family. Just being part of the body of Christ gives us a connection with other believers, but serving in missions with a group of people somehow deepens that bond. Having a common purpose; depending on each other for physical, emotional, and spiritual needs; battling in prayer together; living by faith together; seeing God work through our combined efforts—all this can lead to very special relationships.

Not that all missionaries have perfect relationships with their co-workers—we still have our human, sinful natures that can get in the way, but the potential is great for high-quality relationships. Sometimes you have to work through some "stuff" on the way as you grow up to become more like Christ. Sometimes God allows us to go through lonely times to bring us to depend on Him more and to grow in our relationship with Him. He wants us to listen to Him in ways that we might not if our lives are full of rewarding relationships. But most of the time God has us in relationships with people so that we can meet each other's needs, encourage each other, and work together using our various gifts to accomplish His purposes. Together we are the body of Christ, and that brings a great sense of unity and family.

God has promised to meet our needs. He has promised that if we give up relationships or separate ourselves from family and friends in obedience to Him, He will supply others to fill in the gaps. He is also quite capable of connecting us with a life partner, no matter where in the world He calls us. It is a matter of faith. Is He trustworthy? Gary, Barb, and Mark say yes!

"Lord, I love You. I lay down my need for affection and my fear of failure and disappointing You. I give to You my selfishness and my desire to not be alone."

"My pride, my fear, letting go of my life, my hopes for marriage. Please use me fully, Lord, for Your full glory."

"I offer You my love for children."

"Lord, I give You all the romantic relationships in my life."

"Lord, all of my life I've wanted to be a missionary. I have a family. For some reason Satan has convinced me that the two are not compatible. Please rid me of my fears. I want to obey You alone."

"The burden of my relationship with my girlfriend. Purify our relationship for You. Keep me from fearing the future."

"I give my relationship to you, Father. I won't plan missions and Your calling on my life around my boyfriend."

"Father, I give you my worry and concern for my relationships."

"God, I give to You the fear of loneliness and being a single missionary. I will follow Your plan regardless if I am single or married, for I know that Your will is the best will."

"Lord, I give to You my family and friends whom I love. Let me be willing to give it all up to You. I want to do Your will."

"But Jesus answered the one who was telling Him and said, 'Who is My mother and who are My brothers?' And stretching out His hand toward His disciples, He said, 'Behold My mother and My brothers! For whoever does the will of My Father who is in heaven, he is My brother and sister and mother'" (Matthew 12:48–50).

10

Lack of Faith in God; Doubt

Father, I offer you these things that might limit me from doing my part in seeing the nations worship you . . .

"My fear, Lord, and lack of faith in Your love."

"Fear of giving You my life."

"Lack of confidence in God's will."

"Trusting the Lord with my future."

"My doubt in You, that You are in control."

"Lack of faith, not believing in Your power, fear."

"My lack of trust in the Architect and Contractor of my life."

"My fear of trusting You."

"My own fear of recognizing and admitting the call of the Holy Spirit."

"Lack of faith in what You can do, Lord."

I found it interesting that the number of students who listed "lack of faith in God" as an obstacle was about the same as those who said that they felt unworthy or inadequate. Both obstacles can be overcome by a deeper understanding of who God is and His ability and willingness to work in us, for us, and through us. For some, it is an issue of believing that God is *capable* of doing all that we need Him to do. For most of us, it is more an issue of believing that God is *willing and faithful* to work on our behalf— to guide us, to provide for us, and to give us the power to do what will be expected of us.

Much of our understanding of God comes through the study of His Word as He describes Himself or as we read about how He relates to mankind. We also learn about Him through the testimony of others who know Him and share what they have learned through conversations, teachings, or books. But often the deepest understanding comes when we learn about God firsthand as we allow Him to work in our lives, especially when it involves taking a risk, putting something on the line, and experiencing His intervention or provision on our behalf.

Getting involved in missions is definitely a test of faith, but it is also a great opportunity to stretch and grow your faith as you experience God's faithfulness. If you can take that first baby step forward and see God provide, you will be encouraged to take the next step with a little more boldness.

Juhani and his wife Sari, from Finland, believed in missions and wanted to get involved, but they found that taking the first steps of faith to join a mission agency was difficult. Was God really calling them? Would He really guide them to the right place? Would He actually be able to use them? Would He provide for them? They had to learn to put their faith into action.

A vision for missions was the natural result of growth in our faith. But actually getting into missions was much harder. God spoke to me in various ways but most clearly through Scripture passages like Romans 10. Verses 13–15 make a powerful point:

'WHOEVER WILL CALL UPON THE NAME OF THE LORD WILL BE SAVED.' How then shall they call upon Him in whom they have not believed? And how shall they believe in Him whom they have not heard? And how shall they hear without a preacher? And how shall they preach unless they are sent? Just as it is written, 'HOW BEAUTIFUL ARE THE FEET OF THOSE WHO BRING GLAD TIDINGS OF GOOD THINGS!' (emphasis mine)

Sari had had a vision for missions since her childhood. Then our participation in a two-month mission trip abroad had a strong impact on our lives. It was not easy for us as young believers, but we learned many things about God's work and ourselves. Soon after the summer mission trip was over I was asked to be the youth leader at our church for one year. Without our summer experience, I would not have accepted that position, but now I was willing to do it. I learned many valuable things as I worked with the teenagers. I was leading Bible studies, youth meetings, camps, and worship. It was a good introduction into ministry.

After that one-year commitment was finished I was unemployed for a while, and I felt very low and inadequate. I struggled between God's calling into ministry and a secular job. I had studied to become a graphic designer, but I found that God had given me a new desire to work for His kingdom. The world around me was pressing me to pursue a good career, but that was not my desire any more. Some days I just laid on my bed and wondered, "What is the purpose of my life? Is my life worth living?" This was a difficult time for my wife and me.

During that same time I was hungry for God's Word. Since I was unemployed I had a great opportunity to study the Bible several hours a day. We were also involved in the local church leading some home Bible study groups. That gave us an even stronger desire to be involved in missions. Our local fellowship, however, did not have a focus on missions, so we had to travel seven or eight hours to get in contact with groups who taught about missions.

Little by little we got the impression that our mission field could be the land of Israel. This became clear to us in many different ways. We sang Hebrew songs (we led worship in our meetings), and I was also asked to be the chairman of a group that supported Israel. We started to become more and more interested in Jewish people and their need for the Messiah.

But I needed some confirmation, so we prayed and

we prayed and we prayed. I thought that God would just let us know what to do, so I did not do anything about it for several months. I wondered, "What if I make wrong choices?" Or "Is it just our own idea to go into missions? Maybe it was not God who asked us to go." All kinds of doubts discouraged us almost daily. Both of us had a strong desire to go, but we did not share this with other believers for a long time. I had a narrow view of missions and the way God directs His people. I was waiting for some clear signs, like Gideon with his fleece. Some teaching about God's guidance would have been helpful for us at that time.

Still we felt that this vision was from God and we should pursue it no matter what the cost. Sari urged me to take a step of faith and start contacting mission agencies about possibilities, but I was hesitant. I was still afraid to make decisions. Finally, I took action and phoned a few mission organizations. Some of our contacts were very discouraging. They only asked about our occupations and nothing about our faith or gifts. We were dismayed and astonished that the mission agencies were more interested in our occupations than our spiritual life. But one particular organization seemed more encouraging, especially when I mentioned our interest in Israel. They promised to find out more from the field in Israel and get back to us. Eventually, we got the green light to go. We were so excited about how God confirmed His calling, and we were finally ready to start!

We lived in Israel for over four years and learned many things about evangelism, culture, teamwork, and language. In recent years I have been the field leader here in Finland. We have been with our organization over ten years. We are thankful to God that we stepped out in faith and went, even though we did not know all the details. I think that I was almost like a puppet, just waiting for God to make me move and do everything for me. I learned that I had to take steps of faith and do my part. It is like driving a car: it can only be steered while it's moving. It required obedience and an act of my will, sometimes overruling my feelings and emotions. The confirmation and guidance came only after I started to do my part with faith that God would do His!

Juhani and Sari learned that faith is not passive but active. It was only as they lived out their faith in God by taking steps of obedience that they found the direction they were looking for. They experienced God's faithfulness once they pushed passed their doubts.

James 2 teaches that faith is active and is proven by our actions:

What use is it, my brethren, if someone says he has faith but he has no works? Can that faith save him? . . . Even so faith, if it has no works, is dead, {being} by itself. But someone may {well} say, 'You have faith and I have works; show me your faith without the works, and I will show you my faith by my works.' (vv. 14, 17, 18)

Faith is like a muscle that needs to be exercised in order to grow in strength. The more we use that muscle, the bigger and stronger it becomes and the more it can accomplish. As we take little steps of faith in obedience to God's prompting and find Him faithful to guide us, provide for us, empower us, and use us for His purposes, our faith grows and we are able to trust Him in other ways and for harder decisions.

Taking steps of faith to find out where, when, and how to serve is only part of the journey. Melita from the Philippines found that she also had needs in the areas of finances and personal relationships that required faith in God's ability to provide.

Although I am from the Philippines, I was in Singapore for four years, working as a domestic helper for a Chinese family. Twice a month I had my day off, which gave me the chance to attend church services, seminars, and conferences. In 1991 I attended an international missions convention and was so moved by the great challenge for more workers to go to the mission field that I had to respond. I told my boss, "I will go home to my country and work for the Lord." Four months later I was back in the Philippines.

After attending discipleship lessons I became a key discipler of youth from different churches. But even as I was involved in this effective ministry, the desire to go into missions overseas was always on my mind, yet I just pushed it aside. I kept telling myself, "I am doing well in my present ministry. Besides, I have to reach my Jerusalem first before I go to Samaria and the remote parts of the earth as Jesus commanded in Acts 1:8."

The real reason I was not pursuing missions was my lack of faith that God could use me with my lack of education and training. I also did not know how to go about finding out where to go and had no idea where my financial support would come from. I guess I did not have enough faith that God could overcome these obstacles, so I didn't try.

Ten years later this desire became a burden that I could no longer ignore. I shared this with my brother and sister and my closest friend, and they got excited about it. They encouraged me to trust God and go for it—but *where, how,* and *when?* As I was praying about it my brother came home with a schedule of short-term missions programs that I could participate in locally. I volunteered in one of the programs. While I was involved in this local ministry, the challenge to go outside my comfort zone and reach the unreached people groups in the 10/40 Window once again struck my heart.

As I investigated further I found that there would be missions training in my very own church! I was able to complete the world missions course and learn some creative ways of sharing the gospel. Then we had a chance to apply what we had learned in Baguio City for a day of evangelism. That was followed by two weeks of cross-cultural exposure and ministry to one of the tribal people groups in a mountain province of the Philippines.

During this training I was trying to decide where I should serve overseas. I asked for advice from someone who had previously served with this group and who suggested that I try a particular ministry that involves travel to many different countries. "Okay," I thought. "I'm at peace with that idea. That's what I think God wants me to do." But when I was told the amount of support I would need, I really doubted that I would be able to make it. It was such a large amount! How would I ever be able to raise that?

But this promise kept ringing in my ears: "Where I will lead you, I will provide." I claimed this promise by faith right away, praying fervently about it. I did not know where to find this amount of money, but one thing I did know: God, who has called me, is true and faithful. I only needed to trust and obey Him.

The following day when I visited my sister, she handed me an envelope with more than the amount I needed for my plane ticket. A week later my sister in America sent me some money and promised to support me for two years. Funds kept coming in from unexpected sources. Half of what I needed had been given, but doubt crept in again when I had only two weeks to see the remainder come in. Once again I saw God's provision at the last minute, which seems to be His way of stretching our faith. He used my church, family, friends, and the youths I had previously discipled as instruments to meet this need. I didn't even have to ask them—God motivated them on my behalf. Glory to God for His faithfulness!

Another concern that I learned to trust God with is my future relationships. I want to have a family of my own, and this became an obstacle along the way. While I was preparing to go to the mission field, a friend I greatly admired told me that he liked me and wanted to get to know me better. We shared our plans and visions for the future. I thought, "Oh, this must be the man God will give me as a partner in life and in ministry since we have common goals and visions." But God later showed us that He had different plans for each of us, so it was not to be. Again, I needed to follow God's leading in faith, and, again, I was reminded that He who has called me knows about my needs. Indeed, God showed me His promise in Mark 10:29–30:

Jesus said, "Truly I say to you, there is no one who has left house or brothers or sisters or mother or father or children or farms, for My sake and for the gospel's sake, but that he shall receive a hundred times as much now in the present age, houses and brothers and sisters and mothers and children and farms, along with persecutions; and in the age to come, eternal life."

In every country I go, I meet "parents" I feel close to like the kind and thoughtful Chinese family who hosted me in Malaysia. Others who have become very dear to me are my "moms" in Myanmar and South Africa. When I met these people we became so close to one another, and we continue to correspond with each other. I have also found in many of my team members "brothers" and "sisters" I can confide in who fill my heart with joy and contentment.

As far as a lifetime partner, I have learned to have faith that the Lord knows best. Psalm 139 has been a great encouragement to me till this day. Verses 16 to 18 strongly encourage me not to worry about anything, for a faithful, sovereign Father and God will show Himself to be true. He does not make mistakes. Understanding more about Him and His ways has made me more certain about my future. Even though it is still unknown to me, He has it well planned. I just need to wait on Him in faith, not relying on my own ways and understanding.

Melita has learned that understanding more about God makes it easier to trust Him. Even though she does not know what her future holds, she knows that God, who controls her future, is worthy of her faith and trust.

In case you are thinking that you do not have enough faith to be a missionary, just remember that missionaries aren't the only ones who are required to live by faith. All believers should be living by faith. As Hebrews 11:6 teaches us, "And without faith it is impossible to please Him, for he who comes to God must believe that He is and that He is a rewarder of those who seek Him."

If your faith is weak, I suspect your view of God is too limited. Seek to know Him more deeply, and you will find Him to be faithful, able, and trustworthy (and a lot more!).

"God is big enough to deal with all these things. Lord, I open myself, ask for Your forgiveness, and accept Your will."

"Fear and unbelief that You are totally there for me all the time. You only want my best, which is Your perfect will. Help me to relate more intimately with You."

"Father, I offer You my doubts and fears as a sacrifice so that I may do Your will in the world."

"Lord, I offer my lack of faith and any laziness in doing Your work."

"Lord, I give You my destiny. Open doors for me to serve You. I give You my doubt. Grow compassion within me to lead me to action."

"Lord, I leave to You my selfishness, pride, thinking that I already know everything, and my fear of following You."

"Here I am—do as You will. May I be real. My fears are no longer my problem. I give you my career, schooling, mission area, future husband—my life."

"Sever my safety nets!"

"I have been crucified with Christ; and it is no longer I who live, but Christ lives in me; and the life which I now live in the flesh I live by faith in the Son of God, who loved me and gave Himself up for me" (Galatians 2:20).

"Know therefore that the LORD your God, He is God, the faithful God, who keeps His covenant and His lovingkindness to a thousandth generation with those who love Him and keep His commandments" (Deuteronomy 7:9).

11

Lack of Spiritual Maturity

Father, I offer you these things that might limit me from doing my part in seeing the nations worship you . . .

"My lack of discipline with my personal walk with Christ."

"My judgmental attitude."

"Negative attitudes."

"I need to spend time getting to know the Lord."

"Thinking I know it all."

"My lust and sexual thoughts."

"My own lack of worship and busyness."

"Impatience, laziness, and lack of discipline."

"1. Not coming to You or even thinking of You until I need you. 2. Lustful thoughts, distractions, fantasies. 3. Being an apathetic Christian. 4. Worrying about everything but not doing anything tangible to prevent stuff. 5. Not sharing Your Word."

"I become jealous of Christians who are stronger than me and seem to pray out loud with ease and communicate easily with others—pray for me."

"A need for God's heart to be mine."

"All my plans, all my lusts, all my hang-ups, all my pride."

"Prayerlessness."

"Selfishness, being undisciplined, and needing Christian disciplines."

So many of the issues that showed up on the Wall fall under the category of "lack of spiritual maturity." A majority of the responses included some type of sinful action, attitude problem, or spiritual inadequacy.

Sometimes people think that missionaries are all super-spiritual people—a cut above the rest. Many feel inadequate if they compare themselves with well-known missionaries of history—the martyrs and miracle workers whose biographies we have read or whose stories we have heard. But the fact is that most missionaries are ordinary people who have dedicated their lives to serving God, trusting Him to use them in spite of their weaknesses in obedience to His call. It is true that a certain level of discipline, obedience, and spiritual maturity is important, and churches and mission agencies look for evidence of these things when they consider sending people to serve. After all, the pressures of living cross-culturally and encountering spiritual warfare on the field can be more challenging than living the Christian life at home.

Kathi, an American now serving in South Africa, found that the Lord used her church leadership to help her grow in some areas of spiritual immaturity as she considered joining missions long term. Although it delayed her joining for a time, the results of the process were well worth it:

My first summer missions experience was in Yugoslavia and Hungary in 1986 when I was twenty-six years old. It was fantastic! It was my first experience on an international team and my first encounter with people who did not know anything about Jesus Christ. It was good to learn to share my faith starting from scratch. The leader of this trip challenged me to join this mission group for two years. I felt God was calling me to do this, because I felt such a peace and excitement about this opportunity. I went back to my small, but very missions-minded home church in Nebraska to have the leadership confirm this calling on my life.

The basic reaction I got from the church leaders was that it was a good idea—but they had a couple of hesitations. First, our church had a vision to send out teams, not individuals. They had sent people on short-term outreaches, but they really wanted to send a whole team somewhere to plant a church. Second, they felt that I was not ready to go yet. They wanted to send out leaders, and I was a young, single female. Also, during my university years, although I was a Christian, I went through a period of rebellion against God and His ways. I was still working through these issues, and, though I had made a lot of progress, they did not feel I was solid enough yet to stand firm during difficult times.

I was disappointed but still felt God had called me. I treasured this in my heart and, with the help of the church leaders, grew in my relationship with the Lord in character and in leadership. I joined a team at the church that met weekly and served in the community. I also was discipled one-on-one by two different women in the church. They wanted to train me in leadership, so I started a Bible study and prayer group for girls at our local high school under the mentorship of one of these women. I grew personally, became stronger in areas of personal weakness, and also grew in the ability to lead.

My burden continued for Eastern Europe, especially for Hungary. I already had a degree in biology, but I decided to go back to a university for two years to get another degree in education so I could go to this closed country undercover as a teacher. I also went on two more summer trips.

At one point during this process I had a meeting with the pastors, elders, and their wives—four couples and me. They sensed it was right to begin to plan to send me to Hungary. They openly discussed if I was ready. The pastor asked each one in the group if they felt I was ready. They knew me quite well. In turn each one said yes until it came to the last person, Shelley. She hesitated when she was asked. God had done enough work in my heart that although I was excited about the prospect of going, I was even more interested in growing in the Lord and being in His will. She could not really express what her hesitation was, but I asked her to try. I was a little bit scared but also had a peace in my heart. I knew the Lord was busy burning off the dross of personal ambition in my life, and I was grateful that my desires were conforming to His desires. We had an open conversation in the group. Even though the issues were very personal, I felt comfortable in that I knew they were committed to me and loved me.

The issue Shelley was uncomfortable with was in the area of moral purity. She felt that there was something not quite right in my relationships with men. It was nothing blatant but something subtle in the way I got some of my emotional needs met through these relationships. She wanted to send me out "whole and healthy," both so I would not fall into sin and also so that I could be a leader who would be a blessing to others. We agreed that Shelley would disciple me one-on-one for two years to work through this. We meet weekly for one and a half hours. During the week I did an in-depth Bible study on my own and memorized Scripture. When we met I told her what I was learning. She also asked me tough questions about my thoughts and choices. Shelley held the standard high, and I responded. I also learned about God's grace and mercy.

During this time I started to realize the roots of this problem, and as I faced them the Lord met me there and started the healing process. My father committed suicide when he was eighteen years old and my mother was pregnant with me. Then my stepfather favored his own children over me. Because of my father's suicide, I had to overcome the feeling that God would also leave me. But in His word, God promises us that He will never leave us nor forsake us (Deuteronomy 31:8). I also learned that I was created in my mother's womb, according to God's design (Psalm 139). God had some difficult things planned for me. My biological father was quite a daring young man. I saw that I needed his genes to be brave enough to do what God had created me to do.

When I was twenty-two years old I had reconciled with my stepfather, and now I came to realize that God had a lot to teach me through him too—it just took a while for me to be willing to listen and learn from him. When I looked at my circumstances through earthly eyes, I felt cheated. But when I looked through God's eyes, I felt blessed.

Through Shelly's discipleship I also learned to develop healthy relationships. When I left for full-time service in 1989, I saw how, under pressure, I could have looked to the wrong places to have my emotional needs met. By God's grace, sixteen years later, I have not fallen, I have healthy relationships with my husband, children, and friends, and I am able to lead effectively.

Praise the Lord for people who are willing to speak honestly and to train others so they can send healthy and whole people to the field! I am grateful to the Lord, to Shelley, and to my church leadership who are so committed to me.

The wisdom of Kathi's church leaders and her willingness to submit to their training and timetable paid off—God used Kathi to establish the long-term work in Hungary for her mission agency. God's desire for each of us, whether we are involved in missions or not, is to grow to be more Christ-like, which makes us more useful for His purposes and brings Him more glory. But we are all in process, and He does not require perfection before He is able and willing to use us. All you have to do is look at the lives of people like Abraham, Moses, David, and Peter to see that God can use us in spite of our weaknesses and failures, if our heart is right and we are willing to learn and obey. The importance of our heart attitude is shown in 2 Chronicles 16:9: "For the eyes of the LORD move to and fro throughout the earth that He may strongly support those whose heart is completely His."

Actually, becoming a missionary places you in situations that test your heart and provide many opportunities for growth in spiritual maturity. Each situation you encounter is an opportunity to grow and to see God work in you and through you. Catalina, from Peru, experienced a spiritual "growth spurt" after starting her missionary service:

I came to know Jesus Christ as my Savior eighteen years ago in my home country of Peru. I had been attending a large church where three to four thousand people worshiped together, but when I moved to Italy eight years ago, I ended up in Milan in a little church of only 200 international people. My church in Italy did not have a vision for world missions, at least not at first.

God used a ship to change my church—a ship full of missionaries. They had come to Italy to share the Good News with those who hadn't heard and to help the churches in Italy to grow, both in their outreach to their communities and in their participation in world missions. It was exciting to see my church catch the vision of world missions as we participated in outreaches and programs with the missionaries from the ship. Here were 200 people from more than forty countries around the world living and working together on this ship to spread the gospel. This new vision for world missions that God gave my church had an impact on my life too.

You see, I had already been thinking about serving in missions someday because of my exposure through mission conferences at my church in Peru. In 1999 I attended the Mission '99 conference in Holland with 7,000 young people from all over Europe. During that conference I felt a strong call from God to become a missionary. I decided to give up all my plans and began to seek God's will for my life. To prepare myself I studied English for two months in England and was praying about where the Lord wanted me to serve. When this missionary ship came to Naples, I worked as a volunteer on board, and the Lord spoke to my heart.

I felt that He was calling me to join this ship, and as I talked this over with my church, they agreed. I ended up being my church's first missionary to world missions! I couldn't wait to get to that ship to start serving the Lord and experience the life of a missionary. It was going to be wonderful to live with all those Christians from all over the world and spend my days doing ministry.

It did not take long to find out that my life as a missionary was not going to be so easy. First, I could not pass the English competency test at first, so I was limited in what I could do in work and ministry until my English skills improved. This made me feel left out and frustrated and almost caused me to lose my vision for missions. Also, living on the ship requires everyone to work hard at jobs that need to be done but many times are not very exciting. I had to work many hours doing things like washing dishes, and the heavy lifting caused some inflammation of the muscles in my back, which was painful for months. The glamour of ship life wore off quickly, and I struggled with my attitudes.

I did not understand why everything was so difficult for me. My prayers concentrated on my own needs and desire for happiness, rather than God's will for me. I was so focused on my own struggles and desires that I lost the vision of why I had joined. I became rebellious in my heart, wanting my own way rather than having the desire to serve, which was my motivation for joining.

After four months of struggle, God was gracious to show me my heart. When we were in Norway some of my friends and I took a walk. We ended up on a hill where we prayed, and God brought me to tears as He spoke to my heart. He showed me that my attitude was wrong, and I agreed. I decided right then to place everything in God's hands—and to ask Him to change my heart and my mind and use my life for His glory. I wanted to be an instrument in His hands to be used for His purposes. Finally, I felt joy and His love, and He gave me back the vision of serving Him that I had had in the beginning.

The next day we went out to evangelize, and I had the opportunity to share the gospel with three teenage girls. As I shared I experienced His love, joy, and power. I saw the Spirit working through me. Even though I could not speak proper English, He gave me the right words to share the gospel, and one of the girls prayed to accept Christ.

During this time in Norway I helped to lead three people to faith in the Lord, and it was a real turning point in my life. From then on, in each country we visited, I have seen people receiving Jesus Christ as Lord— Hindus, Catholics, Muslims, Jehovah's Witnesses, and atheists. I praise the Lord for confronting me with my wrong attitudes and changing my heart so that I can be an instrument in His hands and be used for His purposes. Now I can see that He used the difficult things I experienced to teach me to trust Him and to walk in faith and obedience to His word, focusing on Him, no matter what.

As long as we are living on this earth we will be in the process of becoming more of what we should be while struggling with who we are. Do not let the deceiver convince you that you cannot be used by God and get in the way of what God wants to do in and through you. On the other hand, be sensitive and open to the changes that the Lord wants to make in you so that you can grow and mature and be used by Him in the way that He desires. We need to adopt Paul's perspective found in Philippians 3:12–14:

> I don't mean to say that I have already achieved these things or that I have already reached perfection! But I keep working toward that day when I will finally be all that Christ Jesus saved me for and wants me to be. No, dear brothers and sisters, I am still not all I should be, but I am focusing all my energies on this one thing: Forgetting the past and looking forward to what lies ahead, I strain to reach the end of the race and receive the prize for which God, through Christ Jesus, is calling us up to heaven. (NLT)

"Lord, it is my sick and disgusting pride, judgmental attitude, and artificiality that blocks me. My fears, intimidation, and insecurities need to be lost in drunkenness with You so that You can use every ounce of me and my voice and body for You. I do love and thank You."

"My middle-class, white American male, ethnocentric beliefs and values that have been installed into my heart and have corrupted so many of my relationships. Lord, bless me with innocence—that of a child."

"Indecision, lifelong sins (lust, procrastination), trouble building relationships, pride—all these things I give over to You, Lord. Take them and help me to live for You."

"Lord, I give You the sin of lust that is in my life. Thank You for cleaning me. I love You."

"Oh God, help me be obedient."

"Father, nothing is impossible to You. I am weak and sinful if You are not with me, so take me and change me into Your soldier."

"Lord, grow my character. Make it more obedient and serving."

"In this I need help—pornography, pride, self-consciousness. Lord take these from me."

"Lord, I surrender to You my lust, envy, jealousy, and arrogance."

"Prejudices, pride, idols. Jesus, put Your desires in me."

"Lord, I offer You my life as a praise offering. Though I may be set in my ways, impatient and prideful, allow me to truly worship You with my life."

"Lord, help me with lust, anger toward the church, and racism."

"My stinkin' heart—You must radically change my heart!"

"Lord, temptations, afraid of losing control of myself. I pray that I can have a strong conscience."

"All of my thoughts that don't match with You. My feelings that sway with the wind and my lack of desire to spend time in Your Word and in prayer. These I lay at Your feet and pray that You will continue to break and mold me into what You would have me be—whatever the cost."

"For I am confident of this very thing, that He who began a good work in you will perfect it until the day of Christ Jesus. . . . And this I pray, that your love may abound still more and more in real knowledge and all discernment, so that you may approve the things that are excellent, in order to be sincere and blameless until the day of Christ; having been filled with the fruit of righteousness which comes through Jesus Christ, to the glory and praise of God" (Philippians 1:6, 9–11).

12

Need for Guidance or a Sense of Calling

Father, I offer you these things that might limit me from doing my part in seeing the nations worship you . . .

"Unsure about where to go or what specifically to do."

"Not sure how my music can be helpful."

"Personal understanding of my roles."

"I need to see Your love for me and the lost."

"Uncertainty concerning God's direction."

"Has God called me to stay?"

"Understanding God's plan for my life daily."

"Not knowing if it is exactly God's will for me."

"Not knowing the next step."

"Lack of direction, too many opinions, waiting for the perfect opportunity."

"Direction in obeying the Lord's leading to serve Him with my entire being, staying content and dependent on Him in all things and at all times."

For many, one of the obstacles keeping them back from missions was not knowing what God wanted them to do or where He wanted them to go. Was He calling them or not? Sometimes determining God's will seems so tricky. Why can't He just write it on the wall for us?

A friend of mine forwarded to me an e-mail he received that is a beautiful description of how God gently and often subtly guides us. Unfortunately, I could not trace the e-mail back to its author (who knows how many times it had been forwarded!), but I want to share it with you:

GUIDANCE

When I meditated on the word guidance, I kept seeing "dance" at the end of the word. I remember reading that doing God's will is a lot like dancing. When two people try to lead, nothing feels right. The movement doesn't flow with the music, and everything is quite uncomfortable and jerky. When one person realizes and lets the other lead, both bodies begin to flow with the music. One gives gentle cues, perhaps with a nudge to the back or by pressing lightly in one direction or another. It's as if two become one body, moving beautifully. The dance takes surrender, willingness, and attentiveness from one person and gentle guidance and skill from the other. My eyes drew back to the word guidance. When I saw "G," I thought of God, followed by "u" and "i." "God," "u," and "i" dance. God, you and I dance! This statement is what guidance means to me. As I lowered my head, I became willing to trust that I would get guidance about my life. Once again, I became willing to let God lead.

Adele, from Northern Ireland, had to learn how to listen for God's guidance when she became unsure about her future plans. Was God redirecting her through her doubts, experiences, and changing interests? Could He really communicate specifically to her what He wanted her to do?

Being in mission work was not an option I had even considered. I had the stereotypical image of some spinster in her late fifties who had spent her life working among some remote tribe in Africa and came home periodically to share the ups and downs of life on the mission field! Never did I expect that I would end up being a missionary—help us all. God has a sense of humor, that's for sure!

I was brought up in a Christian home and was always a bit rebellious and never wanted to do the norm. I could never see myself settling down into a normal job and having a family.

Leaving school was my first taste of leaving home and hitting foreign shores. I jumped at the chance to work with Chernobyl children in Belarus. Two weeks later when the time was over, in spite of having food poisoning, chicken pox, and being quarantined so I would not infect the kids, I was in love with Eastern Europe. It was like a magnet for me. I did not know that was only the start of God working in my heart.

Going to a university was the logical next step for me. Three years later, after a really enjoyable time of study, I was really getting into the field of linguistics with computing. I wanted to pursue further study and eventually get a well-paid job in a very specialized field. My ideas were uppermost in my mind, and God was never really brought into the equation.

Halfway through the year I talked to my dad about life, the future, and what I saw myself doing. It was only after this conversation that I really began to think seriously about seeking God's will for my life. Before this, God was given a back seat, but then I started to look seriously at my life. I realized that at the end of the day it is only what we have done for Jesus that will have lasting impact. I wanted to know what God had for me.

After this conversation with my dad, I heard my pastor speak from Luke 5:4 where Jesus walks along the beach and tells Simon Peter to "Put out into the deep water and let down your nets for a catch." The pastor challenged us to look at our lives and see if we weren't paddling about by the shoreline and not really going about what God had for us. He challenged us to put our complete trust in God and to launch out in the face of failure and completely unknown circumstances. I responded to that challenge and told God that I was willing to launch out with Him.

Two weeks later I was at an annual Easter conference. When all my friends left to go home after the weekend I felt a strong pull in my heart to stay for the missionary conference. What a meeting! Missionaries from various places were reporting about their work, and one missionary spoke about her work in Brazil. She finished with the same verse from Luke. I knew that was for me and that God was working in my heart. Then the speaker got up and started by saying, "Well, I'd just like to thank one of our missionaries for stealing my text!" I knew what verse he would be speaking from!

All through that sermon I was completely oblivious to everyone else in the place. With tears rolling down my cheeks, I felt as if God was speaking directly to me. It was *so* special, and it was so clear to me that God had something for me that He would show me in His time and in His way. I again responded to the challenge at the end of that meeting, and I was *sure* that God would lead and guide me. He did! Afterwards I found out about a particular agency through a friend. She had some missionaries in her church from Israel, and they just happened to have a leaflet about their work in Russia. I was so interested in the work there that I wrote off for further information. To cut a long story short, I ended up going to Russia on a short-term trip that summer.

I came back completely and hopelessly in love with Russia. I had finished at the university by this stage, and my life was on hold. All my future aspirations to pursue a job in linguistics were put on the back burner. I came home and took a job for a while. After a few months I became so unsettled that I knew something was up. Was God making me like this I wondered? I was in Northern

Ireland, but my heart was in Russia.

I began to look into long-term options for ministry there. Although organizations were eager to have me join, there was a restraining in my heart, and I just knew that this was not what God wanted. I became so confused about God's will and where He was leading me that I was fed up. Maybe it is at times like this that many people give up on the whole idea of missions. I certainly was very close to that point! I hadn't a clue what God wanted from me.

I decided to spend some specific time praying and fasting to discern God's will. I asked God to speak to me specifically, and at the end of that week He did. I was just reading through the Bible as I did every evening. As I turned to the next chapter in Judges, the peace of God just filled my heart when I read chapter 18. The situation with the Danite tribe was the same as my situation, and I nearly laughed at how specific God was! I *knew* that God wanted me to go back to Russia with the same agency. It was clear, and after that I never questioned God's call. I just took Him at His word and went for it.

I have been in Siberia, Russia, for a couple of years and am really enjoying life here. These past years have been some of the hardest of my life, but I can honestly say that I have *never* experienced God like I have during this time. I am looking forward to what He has in store for me this next year!

Sometimes God's guidance is mostly internal, like Adele experienced as God spoke to her heart on numerous occasions. Other times God uses circumstances and "coincidences" to help direct us. Hannah, from the United States, had decided to give only one year to missions before she started college, but the Lord seemed to have other plans. He had some interesting ways of communicating His desires to her.

I am nineteen and came into missions immediately following high school. I served for one year in South Africa, and it was tremendous—life changing in so many ways. I could write pages and pages on that, but suffice it to say that my paradigm was certainly shifted! I had planned to start college after that first year of mission work and applied to four universities in the United States. Strangely enough, all four universities either turned me down or put me on their waiting list, and I was shocked! Coming from an advanced math and science high school, with a very good resume, I should have been accepted easily.

I prayed about other possibilities, and the Lord definitely pointed out in some very interesting ways a ministry called Turning Point in London. As I began praying for some guidance our team in South Africa was traveling to Cape Town for an outreach. There we visited some prisons, and as we were waiting to be released from one particular prison I glanced to my left and noticed a huge poster that read "TURNING POINT." This was referring to a prison program, but what a shock!

Next, as I was reading a book, I stumbled across a line that just seemed to jump out at me: "So Jesus had a *turning point* in his life," and I thought to myself, "What is God trying to say here?"

One of the things that had been drawing me back home was a steady boyfriend, but a few weeks before all this confirmation stuff, he and I decided to just be friends, thus removing one obstacle.

I was praying one night, actually halfheartedly, when I decided to ask the Lord for one more bit of confirmation. After that time of prayer I was going to read a devotional book called *Experiencing God,* which our team was assigned to read as part of our training. I was a couple of months behind in my reading, but when I opened up to the proper page, the title of that day's devotion was "A Turning Point!" On the page below, the phrase "turning point" was mentioned about ten times. I thought to myself, "This is it! God is really telling me something!"

So I called Turning Point and arranged to join them. Besides all the external signs the Lord gave me, the personal confirmation to me was the peace in my heart that this new decision brought.

Within two weeks of that phone call, *all* four universities wrote to say that they had made a mistake, and I was now accepted to attend. Nonetheless, because the Lord had made it so clear, I went to Turning Point. Upon arriving in London, I heard that the Turning Point team had been praying for several months for people to help in the finance office, and I am a bookkeeper. Soon after my arrival a need arose for someone to work with kids and a musician, and that is exactly what I came there to do. God's timing is amazing when I look back at it.

So if God wants you to go somewhere in missions for Him, He will let you know in no uncertain terms. The catch? You have to be listening and available.

As we look for God to guide us we often need to be pushing on doors to see which ones will open. He is quite capable of closing doors and redirecting us as we move forward, always listening for His directions. As we activly seek His direction He will lead us as He promised in Isaiah 30:21: "Your ears will hear a word behind you, 'This is the way, walk in it,' whenever you turn to the right or to the left."

Susanna, from Switzerland, tried pushing on some mission agency doors when she sensed God calling her to a particular type of ministry—but none of the doors would open. Was she mistaken about what she thought the Lord had said to her?

One day I was in the process of having my quiet time when suddenly I had the distinct impression, just as if someone had spoken to me, that I should consider taking a job on the mission field as a school teacher for missionary kids. It was so clear that I could not push it aside. So I began to look around for such a job. I had just turned twenty, and I did not know much about missions. With the help of a friend I found a variety of addresses and began to write to several mission agencies. All of them wrote back nice letters, letting me know that at the moment they would not need any schoolteachers. "I must have misunderstood God," I thought after about the fifth negative reply. "God doesn't really want me on the mission field."

Shortly after this I started to look for a job in a regular Swiss school. In one place I was invited to audition by teaching a lesson for them so that they could see how I work. Only a few days later another youth group from a nearby town invited my youth group to join them for an evening. After the program, while we were having coffee and cake, I talked with a former colleague from a teachers training college. I told her about my experience with the "call." It must have been God leading us to talk together. She told me about a friend who was teaching MKs (missionary kids) in Ivory Coast and who was looking and praying for someone to take over her job. My heart began beating faster!

I spent the next several days praying and wondering what to do. I knew I had the teaching audition for the Swiss school soon and had a good possibility of getting the job. Still, I called the Swiss office of the mission agency that had the MK school in Ivory Coast and told them what had happened. They were very excited that someone was interested in the job in Ivory Coast, and they invited me for a meeting a few days later. We met and talked, and somehow I felt that this could be what God had for me. However, there was still the meeting at the Swiss school. I prayed that the result would be clear.

I did the teaching audition, and it went well. They told me that there was only one other teacher, a woman, who was also being considered. To make a long story short, a week or two later I got a letter from the school, telling me that the job was given to a male teacher. I still do not know where he came from! It was the clear answer I had prayed for. I knew for sure now that my place was to be in Ivory Coast. A few months later I said goodbye to Switzerland and moved to Daloa, Ivory Coast, where I taught six Swiss children from two different mission agencies.

As Adele's, Hannah's, and Susanna's stories show, God guides us in very individual ways. But there are also some common denominators. He spoke to them through His Word. He answered their prayers for direction, and He confirmed His leading with a special peace. Sometimes He used input from other people, sometimes arranged circumstances, but always, eventually, made His will clear. God is not trying to hide His will from us. Sometimes His timing or the need to teach us something through the waiting process leaves us in the dark for a while, but if we are willing to do His will, He will make it known to us.

"Lord, I am unsure of where You would like me to serve—please give me direction. Please grant me wisdom as to whether I should pursue Maritime transportation, business, or politics—all for Your glory!"

"Lord, I give to You my uncertainty of what I should major in, what area of the world I should be in, when and how and with whom I should go. I give to You my finances and my time and trust that You will provide answers and resources in Your time. I give to You my weak, fallible self. I give You the three feet in front of me."

"Father, I desire to know Your calling and will. I love You."

"Heavenly Father, You have me and You hold me. Please continue to lead me with reigns of love. When it is right, take me from the work You have given me to do here and direct my path please."

"Show me!"

"Heavenly Father, I sincerely pray that You will guide me to serving You in the near future and doing Your will in Your name."

"Oh Lord, help me to walk beside You everyday and to hear Your voice."

"Show me where You want me and I will go. Give me courage, take away my fear, pride, self-righteousness ... help me live with the kingdom in mind all the time."

"Good and upright is the LORD; Therefore He instructs sinners in the way. He leads the humble in justice, and He teaches the humble His way. All the paths of the LORD are lovingkindness and truth to those who keep His covenant and His testimonies. For Your name's sake, O LORD, pardon my iniquity, for it is great. Who is the man who fears the LORD? He will instruct him in the way he should choose" (Psalm 25:8–12).

13

Feeling Unworthy or Inadequate

F ather, I offer you these things that might limit me from doing my part in seeing the nations worship you . . .

"My self-consciousness, not finding my identity in Christ."

"Feelings of doubt, inadequacy, and selfishness."

"I'm afraid; I'm not qualified; I'm afraid to start something new and fail."

"Myself, Lord. My fears of not being enough for You, and my fear of not being loveable enough for You."

"My past."

"Quietness, being reserved, not having enough boldness."

"Fear of leaving my comfort zone and fear that I would not be any good or any help. I'm afraid of doing it all wrong."

"Fear that this is a dream I cannot really put faith to. Fear that it is my will, not Your will. Fear that I won't do my best."

"Hurt, anger, loneliness, frustration, being wrong, being right, not being enough, being afraid, being me."

About 10 percent of the responses on the Wall expressed feelings of inadequacy, but I believe we all have times when we doubt God's ability to use us; after all, this is one of the enemy's most effective weapons. If he can get us to concentrate on our inadequacies, our sinfulness, and our past, he can distract and discourage us from following God's plan to use us. Being aware of our limitations and faults is healthy to a point, as it leads us to humility, confession, and dependence on God. He wants us to realize that apart from Him, we can do nothing (John 15:4–5). But feelings of unworthiness that lead to inaction or failure to follow God's leading in our lives is not His desire for us. He asks us to step out in obedience and faith, with the understanding that He will do the work through us if we are available to be used.

Sometimes our feelings of inadequacy stem from our background—cultural, spiritual, or personal messages or impressions we received as we were growing up. Some of us had people in our lives who consistently told us that we would never measure up. Some of us just didn't score well on the tests in our educational system and have accepted labels others put on us.

We need to be able to accept and believe that God designed us with a purpose in mind, and He is capable of using us if we let Him. Ephesians 2:10 assures us of our value to Him: "For we are His workmanship, created in Christ Jesus for good works, which God prepared beforehand, so that we would walk in them."

Peter is a South African who is now leading his mission agency's work in his own country. As a black South African, he had to overcome cultural issues as well as some preconceived ideas of his own before he could see himself serving in missions.

I grew up in South Africa during the height of the apartheid days and became a Christian at the age of twenty. The effect of apartheid on black people has been well documented. In my case there were several obstacles that I faced.

Having been told consistently that I am second class and, therefore, incapable of making a meaningful contribution, I eventually began to believe it. One of my greatest obstacles was believing that I belong to God and therefore am able to accomplish anything through the power of the Holy Spirit.

Also, as I surveyed the mission scene in South Africa, there were few people of color involved in missions, which entrenched my belief that missions was primarily for white people. Because I saw so few black people involved in missions, I assumed that black people were the object of missions. The pictures and slides about missions that I had seen were always of white people ministering to black people.

In my local church in Cape Town, missionaries would come and share their experiences once a month on a Thursday evening. Most of the people who came fit my caricature of a "missionary"—predominantly older people of Caucasian origin, showing slides of themselves reaching out to the poor, backward people of Africa. They would take twenty minutes to talk about two slides and were generally boring. My impression was that mission work was to be avoided at all cost, especially if one was young.

My other impression was that one almost had to belong to the Christian faith "hall of fame" to become a missionary. Missionaries had to show no weaknesses and had to be people of exceptional quality.

Because so few people were involved in missions in my local city, I came to the conclusion that we first need to sort out our problems at home before we should think of the world. All around me I saw needs, and I became very introspective and inward looking.

I had studied at a Bible night school for four years and was very involved in my local church. I was one of the youth leaders of about 250 young people. I became an itinerant preacher within the city. I felt I was doing my bit for God and began to feel very comfortable. Besides, I had just started working and was beginning to earn fairly good money. Having money in my pocket gave me a great sense of security. It meant that I didn't need to be dependent upon anyone else.

I remember well the day after writing my final exam at the University of South Africa. I was praying through the book *Operation World,* and I remember praying for a particular country. One of the prayer points was to ask the Lord of the harvest to send forth laborers. I remember clearly that when I prayed that prayer, I was challenged personally to be part of the answer. All of the excuses that I had up to that point came into question.

About that time a mission ship visited Cape Town. As I attended a youth leaders conference on board, all of my ideas about the kind of people who get involved in missions were blown away. I saw young people who were as fallible as I am but who had zeal to know and serve the Lord. I kept thinking, "If they can do it, then so can I."

I remember sharing my vision to join missions with the leaders of my local church. Although this was something foreign to them, they could see how seriously I viewed this call upon my life. As I took time to walk through the process with them, they became convinced of the missionary call upon the local church as well. Even though my family and community were quite poor and despite all the financial challenges that faced the church, they agreed to support me.

Marcia, from the United States, believed that God was calling her to missionary service, so she decided to attend a Bible school to help her prepare herself. She started out feeling very inadequate, but through good teaching and studying some important passages of Scripture, she learned some great lessons about where our adequacy for mission service comes from.

During a chapel message at Moody Bible Institute, a speaker shared her incredible personal story of missionary life, basing it in Paul's powerful words:

For God, who said, "Let light shine out of darkness," made his light shine in our hearts to give us the light of the knowledge of the glory of

God in the face of Christ. But we have this treasure in jars of clay to show that this all-surpassing power is from God and not from us. (2 Corinthians 4:6–7, NIV)

When the speaker asked whether God might be calling some of us to the Lord's work in the world, I resisted, realizing that such a commitment would change my life. I did not want to creep "out of my comfort zone" as George Verwer describes it, but mainly I was afraid. I squirmed a lot. "Who me? Go overseas?" I may have even paraphrased Moses' memorable words: "O Lord, please send someone else to do it" (Exodus 4:13). I knew I was a jar of clay.

I was not afraid of the typical things people fear about living in another country. New languages, new people, new customs, new ideas, new food, new friends—that was the easy part, an interesting adventure. Instead, I feared that I did not have what it took to be an effective witness for the Lord. I knew that I did not love the Lord my God with all of my heart and strength and soul, nor did I love my neighbor as myself. I knew that I was self-centered and not always sensitive to the needs of others. I knew that I did not like to step on people's toes or offend, so how could I push Jesus on them? I did not have a "heart for the lost" like I should have. I doubted whether I could stand up under hardship or persecution. I did not pray enough. It all boiled down to a deep sense of inadequacy. Since I could never seem to do enough or be good enough, how could I have the audacity to be an ambassador for the Lord in another country? I was sure I would be a failure.

Along with the jars of clay message, Jesus' teaching about the vine and the branches changed my heart in a profound way. Before I had read John 15 from the perspective of fear and guilt. In my eyes I was unfruitful compared to other Christians, so any day God might chop me off and throw me out. I tried not to think about burning in fires. I struggled to remain in Christ and felt that I was a failure. If only I could have steady quiet times, win one person to the Lord a week, and practice the fruit of the Spirit in the way that other believers seemed to. My salvation, I knew, was based on grace through faith, not works. But as a sincere, seeking Christian, the Bible had a lot of texts that challenged me and shook me up when I read them without any theological blinders.

Years later, with wise counsel, I realized that many of those feelings came from inaccurate psychological perceptions I had held since childhood and from an incomplete understanding of God's love and my identity in Christ. In Christ, "there is now no condemnation" (Romans 8:1, NIV). On the other hand, the Holy Spirit does bring conviction, not for condemnation, but to move believers forward. I had an accurate picture of myself as an inadequate person, deeply in need of the Lord's grace in my life. But I needed a better understanding to avoid the quagmire of self-condemnation.

In my misguided thinking I had utterly failed to understand the main point of John 15. The solution did not lie in me and all my earnest self-improvements. The solution was tied to the mystery of remaining in Christ. "Remain in me, and I will remain in you. No branch can bear fruit by itself; it must remain in the vine. Neither can you bear fruit unless you remain in me" (John 15:4, NIV). The transformation to fruitfulness was a process that took time. God, not I, was the only one able to produce or judge the quality of fruit in my life, and it would be something different and unique, according to how God designed me. Abiding in Christ was not an amalgamation of works but a decision of the will to recognize that I need the Lord and His grace for everything I do: "Apart from me you can do nothing" (John 15:5, NIV). As a believer my acceptance in the Lord was something that I could rest in. From that stronghold flowed my confidence and security to love the world. My acceptance doesn't start from the opposite end—that I do all these wonderful works, somehow proving how committed a disciple I am, like gluing an artificial apple onto an apple tree.

From that new understanding of remaining in Christ, I was able to explore missionary work by taking smaller steps. I went on two spring outreaches to Native American tribes and later on a summer training trip to China, Hong Kong, and Indonesia. At another altar call I said yes to whatever future God had for me, trusting it would be something I could do or, more accurately, something He could do through me.

I call remaining in Christ a mystery because for me that concept has been learned and applied through time, particularly during the last eight years of my life in Croatia. I doubt I would have learned about remaining in Christ as deeply if I had not been willing to go. It was like learning to scuba dive. All of the above-water activities I had enjoyed as a swimmer never prepared me for the wonder of another world just below the surface. Nothing had changed except my perspective and a new way to breathe.

One new perspective I gained in Croatia was seeing how my family and I were a part of God's grand design through the body of Christ. God was the Architect and Builder of a plan to build His church in Istra, Croatia. We were a hammer, a chisel, a nail, a jar of clay. There is something glorious and humbling in that. It was glorious because we so clearly saw our purpose for that time. Our life counted and our ministry was important. But we were not the hinge of the whole enterprise. God was using us and many other believers from all over the world to pound in a nail or chisel out a wall in order to build a new arm of the body of Christ in an unreached area. God was doing it. My family, our team, our church, other missionaries, and other believers praying throughout the world were all a part of it. I understood, then, that fruit in a person's life was not an individual effort but a natural outgrowth of the living body of Christ working together. He is the vine. We are the branches. The true fruitfulness flows from Him through us, and we have the delight to see the fruit on the other end.

As a jar of clay I may have cracks, blemishes, and glaring imperfections. God, however, is working those out and can use me in the meantime. There is no arrival point a Christian must reach before she is worthy to be a branch bearing fruit. There is only remaining in Christ.

Marcia's story illustrates how important it is to understand biblical truths about who we are in Christ and where our ability to serve God effectively comes from. When we understand that we are merely the channels through which God works as we allow

Him to use our lives, the pressure is taken off of us to perform.

"Terri," from South Africa, felt she had an excuse for not going into missions. She had been born deaf, and her education had discouraged her from learning sign language. But after her salvation she felt the Lord calling her to serve in a sensitive country that we will call "Tridon" for security reasons. But how could she be used with her disability?

During my years of study, I met a man who was deaf and relied totally on sign language. After getting to know him and getting involved in the South African Deaf Christian Community, I began to accept my deafness as well as learn the importance of sign language, realizing that this is a special culture all its own.

When I completed my studies and started working as a draftsman, I met a number of believers who were mission-minded, and through them I heard about opportunities to serve. For years I had supported missionaries but never considered going myself. I never wanted to leave my job, which I enjoyed, nor my fellowship, my family, and, particularly, my friends. When people asked me to consider serving on a short-term mission trip, my deafness provided a really good excuse. But then the Lord used Exodus 4:10–12 to touch me deeply:

Then Moses said to the LORD, "Please, Lord, I have never been eloquent, neither recently nor in time past, nor since You have spoken to Your servant; for I am slow of speech and slow of tongue." The LORD said to him, "Who has made man's mouth? Or who makes him mute or deaf, or seeing or blind? Is it not I, the LORD? Now then go, and I, even I, will be with your mouth, and teach you what you are to say."

I decided to join a month-long outreach in South Africa headed by a mission agency. During that time the Lord made it clear that I should join this mission agency for a longer period, so I joined for a year of training.

Tridon became a real burden on my heart during that year. I struggled with this, not knowing what I would do there. Being deaf and relying totally on lip-reading when I did not know the language was a big step to take. To walk into another culture and not know what life would be like there was scary. I knew in my heart I was called to Tridon, but others thought I was absolutely crazy! Even Christian friends and family encouraged me to give up the idea as they felt I wouldn't cope. Their concerns and disapproval made me feel unworthy. I felt I would fail, and it made me more anxious. I started to see how hard it would be to leave my job and comfort zone, where I felt understood and could understand those I could clearly lip-read, but I still felt convinced that He was calling me to Tridon.

I applied to serve there in spite of my fears, and about that time a family from Tridon came to train us for a few months. They were such an encouragement to me, and then I was accepted to serve in Tridon by the mission team there! The Lord used many circumstances and Scriptures—too numerous to share—to confirmed my calling to this country.

I joined the Tridon team and noticed deaf people walking about during the outreaches. One day I asked where all the deaf people get together. This was the start of our "deaf ministry"—developing contacts and identifying with this tight community. Since then we have been researching, reaching out, and discovering that there are a surprising number of deaf people in this land (more than 10,000 people).

The Lord has also brought me into contact with other believers who share the same vision. We have been attending deaf clubs in various cities to befriend and build relationships. There has already been fruit from our labor, and several friends have accepted Jesus as Lord and Savior. A Bible study for the deaf has been established, and we are developing this ministry further. We recently began the Deaf Project, a vision the Lord gave me for an activity center for the deaf.

This will help the deaf by building up their confidence, teaching them skills, and most of all, showing them unconditional love and acceptance. This "friendship evangelism" will hopefully be a wonderful bridge of reconciliation between the deaf and hearing world, leading them to a place of trusting and accepting the Lord! It is my desire that other disadvantaged people come to experience the incredible blessing of knowing the Lord like I have. Deaf people need to hear the gospel, and I want to be one of God's channels to reach them.

I want to be His hands and His feet, reaching out in His name and knowing certainly that the work He is doing is not because of any great ability I have but only because in my weakness He is strong. God does not need perfect people to accomplish things but those willing to use whatever they have been given for His purposes. As I see how God uses my hearing disability to reach the deaf in Tridon, I realize I am definitely useful! God has a specific plan for me and has turned my disability into an ability He is using!

Peter, Marcia, and Terri all learned that although they felt inadequate to serve, if they were willing to allow God to work through them, in spite of their limitations, He could use them. If He calls us, He will empower us. It is not about us; it is about Him.

"God, I offer You my fears, my inadequacies, my hopes, and my pain. Take all that I am, the good and the bad, and do whatever it takes that You may be glorified in me. I surrender. I give You my heart."

"Lord Father, I need more confidence and boldness to speak Your word to others."

"Lord, please rescue me from my fear of approaching strangers, especially with the gospel, of thinking big and failing, that I will keep stumbling and falling over my weaknesses."

"Fear of failure and of saying the wrong things. Lord, I need confidence that You will give me wisdom in ministering to those You have placed in my life."

"Lord, I offer my inhibitions, my fear of my parents, my future, my self-consciousness. Lord, I offer You my fear of unknown cultures, my ignorance. Please free me of self and empower me by Your Holy Spirit. Help me to see a little more of the vision You have for me and this world. Help me not to hold back any longer."

"Lord Father, I give You my fears and tears, my inability, my inhibitions, they are in Your hands. Your will be done. I give You my moments of stubbornness, and I give You my futile heart that gets weary; let it not be so! Give me perseverance. God, I give You any sin I have, and I repent. I give You my pride, and I put all of my confidence in Christ!"

"And He has said to me, 'My grace is sufficient for you, for power is perfected in weakness.' Most gladly, therefore, I will rather boast about my weaknesses, so that the power of Christ may dwell in me. Therefore I am well content with weaknesses, with insults, with distresses, with persecutions, with difficulties, for Christ's sake; for when I am weak, then I am strong" (2 Corinthians 12: 9–10).

14

Schooling and Training

Father, I offer you these things that might limit me from doing my part in seeing the nations worship you . . .

"I'm pressured to get my degree."

"Caught up in ambition and school."

"College degree."

"I'm waiting for God's timing regarding finishing school, finances."

"My fear that I don't have anything to serve people with."

"Preparation and when and how."

"Lack of knowledge and ability."

Requirements for schooling and training vary greatly throughout the mission world. Some organizations require Bible school, if not seminary training, while others have no formal school requirements but give you training on the field. Some have extensive training for years in the United States before they let you go overseas, and others send you to the field very quickly. Some fields have established schools with formal training, and others are more "hands on, learn as you go" with the help and training of experienced missionaries. Obviously, some missionary occupations require specific training, like doctors, pilots, or Bible translators.

What will be required of you will depend on what you are called to do and what mission agency you desire to serve with. Sometimes the Lord leads you through a path of training that He has designed specifically for you, to suit the purposes He has planned for you, before you even know where He wants you to serve.

Ruth, from the United States, spent a summer traveling across the States with an evangelistic team. She had a great experience and believed she wanted to continue in some type of missionary service, but how should she prepare? One step at a time the Lord led her through a process that eventually prepared her for His plan.

Once my first short-term mission trip was over I thought, "If God is leading me in this direction, I need some training." My first step was to attend a discipleship training school. This involved six months of training with one month in Mexico working among the local churches. This was my first cross-cultural experience. I was scared and didn't know any Spanish, yet I was strangely drawn into this work. One special event was when we attended a church worship service. It was all in Spanish, and I understood nothing! But the worship time was awesome and full of life. After the meeting an older woman came up to me and put her hand on her heart and then on my heart. She raised her hands toward heaven and gave me a huge hug. I was so impressed by her act. It showed me that languages do not bind the spirit of God. I began to warm up to the idea of working overseas—especially if I met loving people like this woman.

I figured if I were truly going to work overseas, I should get some preparation. Everyone I knew who served God overseas was in my eyes a highly educated person—with an undergraduate and graduate degree in theology, medicine, or education. I had struggled with my academic inabilities in high school. How could God use someone like me to serve in another country? I could not read well, I was not a good speaker, I hated to be in front of a class, and I preferred to be last rather than first to answer a question.

Now there seemed to be a nudge, telling me to go ahead and step out, saying, "Trust God, you can do it!" I argued with God. I tried to make excuses: Bible school takes four long years; I want to get to the foreign field now if that is where the Lord is leading me. Peace only came to my heart as I assured myself that four years is not a long time. I should take the time to be equipped for my call. I did want to follow Jesus, but go to college? I decided to test the waters. I would apply to Bible school, and if they did not accept me I would know it wasn't God's will. But surprisingly, they did accept me.

The classes at Bible school were just what I needed. I found a new fascination for the Old Testament. The missions and evangelism classes were challenging and demanding, with all the memorization, but later I realized how valuable those Scripture passages were to my daily life. The doctrine classes were revealing as I learned about the different doctrinal beliefs. At school we had the opportunity to not only study and work on the campus but also to take part in outreach ministries. All these areas shaped my life more than I could imagine. It is one thing to know God's Word but another to live it and to explain God's truths to others who have never heard them.

The second missions conference I attended at school was extremely influential in giving me direction for my future ministry. The speaker challenged us to go to the unreached peoples. The Scripture he used was Romans 15:20–21, "It has always been my ambition to preach the gospel where Christ was not known, so that I would not be building on someone else's foundation. Rather, as it is written: 'Those who were not told about him will see, and those who have not heard will understand'" (NIV).

As I listened to the heart of this speaker, these verses became my heart's ambition—to go to unreached people. Shortly after the conference, I met a team planning to work in Honduras. I checked it out according to my mandate: it was a new work, a new region, and it would not build on another man's foundation. I prayed about joining the team, and it seemed right. I thought to myself, "I am going to Honduras to reach the Honduran people with the gospel!" My heart was at peace as I considered my upcoming year of internship.

I was assigned to a particular mission agency's headquarters for my internship. It was during this time that I was challenged to work in the Muslim world. A man told me that less than 2 percent of overseas workers work in the Muslim world. I was planning on working in Honduras. Therefore, when I first heard about the need in this part of the world, I just pushed it aside. But much to my amazement, during my year of internship, working in a literature room of Muslim books, God began to stir an interest in my heart to reach the Muslim people with the love of Christ

My internship was great. Not only did I meet new candidates taking classes and preparing to go overseas, but returning missionaries would also come and share their hearts with their home mission and I was able to listen in. We also had weekly prayer meetings that enabled me to learn about many of the obstacles missionaries were facing on the field. I could not have picked a better place to broaden my horizon.

I returned to school for my final year of studies. It was a great opportunity to talk openly about the struggles that my classmates and I faced on our internships and to find solutions. Shortly after returning to school, I heard that the work in Honduras no longer existed. God clearly closed the door. As I began asking God, "Now where should I go?" He brought to my memory the need among the Muslim peoples. "Lord, are you calling me to Asia?" When I asked my school leaders about joining a team I had heard about in South Asia, they encouraged me to go.

That was twenty years ago. Those preparation years at discipleship training school, Bible school, my year of internship, and then my hands-on training on the field were life changing. It was good to take each transition step-by-step rather than running ahead. For me this was the best way to prepare myself for serving the Lord overseas.

I have also learned that it is beneficial to take a sabbatical year to study, improve my abilities, and learn new ways to minister to the people God has called me to. After working in South Asia for seven years, I attended Northwestern College and completed a social science degree. My advisor there encouraged me to complete a master's degree, but my heart was set on returning to South Asia and the work there. Besides, it had been an intensive two years of studies, and I was ready for a break. Now, ten years later, I'm working on a master's in linguistics. God is opening new doors for me, and as I walk forward, those doors are staying open. Jesus wants each of us to learn the security and joy of following Him. He takes us in our weakness, encouraging us to trust and follow Him. He will take us deeper in our relationship with Him and use us in ways we never thought possible.

Ruth's story shows that our training often is ongoing. It is not uncommon, after a few years on the field, for missionaries to come back for more training or education. They might see special needs they could fill if they had a particular degree or a new ministry that could be developed with some specific training.

Some students decide to give a year or two to missions before they even start college. That is what Hannah from the United States decided to do. In fact, after the one year she intended to give, she decided to stay for a second. Here are some of the pros and cons from her perspective:

After a year of missionary service in South Africa, I was excited but not at peace about going back to college in the States. I felt God was leading me to stay in missions for at least one more year, but I was fearful. Taking one year off after high school is one thing, but my friends and relatives were pretty jumpy at the thought of me continuing with mission work instead of getting into college. Maybe more than anyone else, I was afraid of taking a road less traveled. Was it really the right choice?

I was worried that I would eventually go back to the States to start college and be a "missionary misfit." I would be a few years older than my classmates with a different worldview, experiences, and morals that would set me apart in an awkward way. But at the same time I knew that my foundation as a Christian had been strengthened and that I would be more prepared to face the world with a better understanding of myself.

Now that I have finished my two years of missionary service and have been in college, I have found that I am not a misfit after all. I actually feel better prepared to disciple and encourage my brothers and sisters in Christ because of my experiences, and I find myself recruiting my friends into missions. Everyone, whether Christian or not, enjoys hearing my missionary stories. The fact that I am a few years older than my classmates has actually turned out to be a blessing.

I am of the opinion that there is a place and a time for college and university, but a year or two off will undoubtedly teach you more about who you are, who God is, and how you can actively serve in God's kingdom.

By the time Hannah finished her first couple of years in mission service, she may have had a better idea of what she wanted to do with her life overall. She may have been better prepared to make decisions about what kind of degree she wanted to pursue, perhaps so she could go back to serve long-term somewhere.

Like so many other areas of the Christian life, the path the Lord leads us on in preparation for His service is usually unique and custom-made according to His plans for us. Karl, from the Czech Republic, found that God kept redirecting him through the advice of others and circumstances. The process was not quick or direct, but it was just what Karl needed to prepare him for the mission field.

When I was eleven years old my family had to leave Czechoslovakia for political reasons. We emigrated to West Germany where I suffered through my teenage years, not really fitting in and finding materialism did not satisfy a deeper hunger in my life. Convinced by a popular youth magazine that I needed a girlfriend, I ended up going to a Christian youth group with my sister in order to meet girls. I did not believe in the existence of God, but since I could not find a girlfriend at the disco, I thought this would be a good place to meet someone.

At the meeting I heard a missionary, who had been working in West Africa for ten years, give his testimony. Afterwards he prayed along with several of the young people. This was all new to me. I was confused because I did not believe in God, but these kids had something I was missing. For a year I attended this group, asking questions and learning about Jesus. I finally asked God to prove His existence by specifically answering several prayers. He did, and I gave my life to Him.

A year later I had my first mission experience during Easter break. Not only did I learn more about God and missions, but I also experienced the joy of being used by God to lead others to Him. A year after that I felt God call me into missions at a youth missions conference. I was ready to stop my education and professional training and go, but the man who counseled me advised that it would be better to go into missions with a profession. He said I should finish my schooling and training first, which was good advice. In the meantime I participated in mission outreaches during Easter and summer breaks.

Two years later, after having finished my training, I went to enroll in Bible school. The leader there suggested that I get my mandatory military/civil service out of the way before attending Bible school. I was assigned to spend my eighteen months of civil service in a hospital. "Good," I thought, "I can minister to the patients." But I was assigned the duty of collecting bags of trash throughout the hospital and burning them in the cellar.

At first I struggled to understand why God had me in this situation—to preach to bags of trash? But soon I saw His wisdom as I was able to build relationships with the doctors and nurses, whom I saw regularly, and to start a Bible study with them. I also became the youth leader for the local Catholic youth group (as a Protestant!). It was a good time for me to learn about stepping out in faith and developing my own ministry opportunities.

Once my civil service was complete, I again looked into attending Bible school. My parents, who were not believers, wanted me to pursue the career I was trained for, but when they saw my determination to become a missionary and then learned that the Bible school was world-renowned and in a beautiful Swiss location, they agreed. Three years later I finished school and wrote to various mission organizations, looking for an opportunity to serve.

I was surprised when I received no response at all! Almost weekly missionaries had come to our school, asking for people to join their fields, but now when I was ready to go, nothing. I was also surprised when my denomination in Germany asked me to come and be a preacher in Black Forest. I accepted and worked there for six years. Looking back now I can see it was good preparation for the work I later did in missions—working with children and youth, ministering in camps, and training lay leaders and pastors. It was also where I met my wife, through a special six-month evangelism program. For me it was love at first sight, but all the members of the team had agreed to a non-dating policy. It was hard to wait until the end of those six months to tell her how I felt, but about a year later we were married.

Eventually, we began to sense it was time for a change—time to follow our original plans to go into missions (she had felt called before we met too). We were invited to serve in Belgium and were making plans to go there when the "Velvet Revolution" occurred in Czechoslovakia. A student demonstration led to the overthrow of the communist government, and the new government left the country open to ministry.

Our plans changed quickly, and we soon found ourselves in Czechoslovakia, my home country, figuring out how to start a ministry there. I was grateful for the ministry experience I had gained previously but also challenged as I had to do several things I had never done before—starting a mission organization, leading an international team, and organizing major evangelistic campaigns—all during the first year!

Now we have been serving in the Czech Republic for thirteen years. It took a few years from the time I felt the call to mission to get through all my schooling and God's training program in Black Forest, Germany, but God knew what He was doing. I would not have been as prepared for what I needed to do in the Czech Republic without all of those experiences.

God's plan for Karl's training involved several years, including both Bible school and hands-on ministry, before going into missions. But sometimes God leads in a more radical way and asks someone to just go for it—now! Ray, from the United States, had come to Christ as an adult and started seminary right away so he could be effective in sharing the gospel. But his passion could not seem to wait for his graduation, and he felt the Lord cheering him on.

I had been at Fuller Seminary for one and a half years when appeals from different mission agencies began to get to me. Most groups would encourage me to finish my seminary training before applying. However, one group, inspired by their founder C. T. Studd's dictum, "Give me a man whose heart is on fire for God and for lost souls, and any old cabbage will do for a head," encouraged me to apply immediately.

I had not gotten their acceptance letter when the semester was coming to a close, but I told the seminary I would not be returning the following semester. After reading Revelation 3:8 ("I know your deeds. Behold, I have put before you an open door which no one can shut; because you have a little power, and have kept My word, and have not denied My name."), I decided to follow the advice of the previous verse, "And to the angel of the church in Philadelphia write," since the mission agency's headquarters was outside Philadelphia at Fort Washington. So I wrote, saying that I believed the Lord had set before me an open door and was about to leave seminary to join then.

When I arrived they seemed somewhat surprised, but they decided they would accept me on trial. After three months they agreed to accept me as a candidate. That was in the spring of 1959, just two years after my conversion. It is marvelous how in "forsaking all," I saw the Lord faithfully supply all my needs. And now, forty-four years after my conversion, I can affirm He has proven faithful in supplying all my needs all these years. At age seventy-four I have no reason to doubt His faithfulness or to fear that He will leave me in the lurch at the end. Yes, God has been good to me!

The uniqueness of each of these stories shows, again, that God works with each of us as individuals. There is not one right way to prepare for missions. Requirements will vary, as will the opportunities for growth and experience along the way. Schooling and training are not really obstacles but opportunities for God to prepare us for what is ahead. Even during formal schooling there are opportunities for short-term mission trips like those in which Karl was involved. Ruth discovered that internships provide opportunities for ministry as well as valuable experience and even redirection of future plans. Hannah found that God could use her even before she started college and learned things about herself, God, and the world that she might never have learned in a classroom. Through Ray we see that sometimes just going and learning along the way is an option. The key is to be sensitive to what the Lord is leading you to do.

———————————

"Dear Lord, I give to you my inability to give my schooling to you and my fear of the future."

"Father God, I confess that I am too prideful. I sometimes think that I can't possibly do the things You want me to—that I am not experienced or don't have the ability. Break me of that God. Break me of my selfishness in wanting to do what I want. I pray that You will mold me into the woman You want me to be. Thank you for Your love and forgiveness and grace."

"Lord, I need to know your timing for missions, school, and the future."

———————————

"All Scripture is inspired by God and profitable for teaching, for reproof, for correction, for training in righteousness; so that the man of God may be adequate, equipped for every good work" (2 Timothy 3:16–17).

"Be diligent to present yourself approved to God as a workman who does not need to be ashamed, accurately handling the word of truth" (2 Timothy 2:15).

15

Finances

Father, I offer you these things that might limit me from doing my part in seeing the nations worship you . . .

"Financial concerns."

"God, I have $ problems."

"Financial support."

"Thinking that I need to prepare more money."

"$ is a problem if I let it be, but God provides!"

"My family's financial problems."

"Financial incapability right now."

"$24,000 in school debt, lack of faith and direction."

"My debts, student loans, education bill."

"Having to drop my pride and ask others for financial support."

Most mission agencies require their missionaries to raise financial support. For many people this is the biggest obstacle. In our society that values independence and financial security, asking people to give their money to provide for our needs is uncomfortable and, for some, incomprehensible. Why would anyone give his or her hard-earned money to support you? Perhaps out of obedience to God, as Paul instructed in 2 Corinthians 9:7–8, 11, 13:

> Each man should give what he has decided in his heart to give, not reluctantly or under compulsion, for God loves a cheerful giver. And God is able to make all grace abound to you, so that in all things at all times, having all that you need, you will abound in every good work. . . . You will be made rich in every way so that you can be generous on every occasion, and through us your generosity will result in thanksgiving to God. . . . Because of the service by which you have proved yourselves, men will praise God for the obedience that accompanies your confession of the gospel of Christ, and for your generosity in sharing with them and with everyone else. (NIV)

When we gather a support team for our ministry, not only are we providing our supporters with an opportunity to obey the Lord by giving, but they also receive a reward for their generosity:

Even when I was in Thessalonica you sent help more than once. I don't say this because I want a gift from you. What I want is for you to receive a well-earned reward because of your kindness. At the moment I have all I need—more than I need! I am generously supplied with the gifts you sent me with Epaphroditus. They are a sweet-smelling sacrifice that is acceptable to God and pleases him. And this same God who takes care of me will supply all your needs from his glorious riches, which have been given to us in Christ Jesus. (Philippians 4:16–19, NLT)

When we understand that raising support is not simply asking people for money but rather giving them an opportunity to be a part of God's ministry through their partnership with us, we can feel better about it. It is not our job to convince them—God will do that. And as they obey His prompting, they receive the joy of giving and the blessing of God providing for their own needs.

Sometimes support comes through individuals—friends and family who are behind us and want to participate in ministry through us. Our local church is also key in the process of sending us out—helping us to grow spiritually, determining our readiness, confirming our call, and providing prayer and financial support.

Seija, from Finland, felt a clear call from God to a particular mission opportunity during her denomination's annual mission conference one summer. Even though she was fairly new and unknown at her church, she found that God had prepared the way for her.

I left the conference with an assurance that it was God's will for me to join a particular mission team. I knew that I should share what had happened with my church and see what they thought about it. That summer had been special: I had gotten to know people from my church while doing my internship there. I had joined the church a year earlier, but because I had been away most of the year at college I had not gotten to know people and they did not know me. When I looked for a place to do my internship, my home church had been my last choice. When all the other options did not work, I ended up going home. I am so thankful that God knew better!

When I went to my church's prayer meeting the week after the conference, I prayed that I would have an opportunity to share what I had experienced. That was the only meeting the whole summer where people were asked to come up and share! I shared what had happened to me at the conference. Later our children's worker came to me and asked me to write a letter to the elders and missions board. It turned out that the missions board was quite desperate, because the family they had been supporting had come back from their field and was not planning to return. Now they had nobody to support. My church ended up providing my full support—and all that happened a year before I actually joined!

So many times we can look back and see how God has orchestrated the details of our life to accomplish His plans, like arranging for Seija to do her internship at her home church. There she built relationships, experienced God's call into missions, and then was able to share her support need with the missions committee which was looking for a missionary to support.

Kenny, from Singapore, had a similar experience of God directing his steps to a church that would support him. As a brand-new Christian he had a desire to serve and ended up with a job in a drug rehabilitation center. But when he found a place he wanted to serve in missions, he realized his need for a church to send him.

Being a new Christian and growing up spiritually in a drug rehab-center where I was serving did not give me much of a church background. I told my leader about my intention to become a missionary and my need for church support. He arranged for me to become a member of a local church about a ten-minute walk from my place. Sunday came, and I went to this church. I had prayed that the Lord would lead me to the right church. I did not have any peace about this one, so I took a twenty-minute bus ride and went to another church that I had visited when I was a young man. When I arrived I knew it was the right church.

At the first prayer meeting I attended at this church, I was asked to give my testimony and to share a prayer request. I shared about my desire to join missions and asked that they pray for me. They were excited because they had prayed for thirty-six years to send out a missionary, and they had no one to send. They had a missions committee and a missions budget but no missionaries. This church sent me out after being a member for only four months. They decided to provide my full support plus pay for my airfare. They have been supporting me for the last twenty-two years.

Seija and Kenny both experienced God's full provision through their home churches, but many missionaries do not receive their whole support, or even a significant part of it, from their church. Many raise much of their support through the generosity and faithfulness of individuals who partner with them in ministry by sending financial support and praying for them. Jennie, from England, realized that individuals would have to make up her support team, but when she looked at her list of potential supporters she thought it looked pretty hopeless.

When God started calling me to missions, it took me a very long time to listen. I had left college with an honors' degree and excellent references and was looking for a teaching job. After months of applications, interviews, and near misses, I gave into the "still small voice" and wrote to a missions group for information about teaching positions they had.

When the information pack arrived a few days later, I looked through it and was horrified to learn that I would have to raise personal support. I thought through my list of family and friends. Many had just left college as I had and were struggling to pay off student loans. Some were newly married and taking on the responsibilities of mortgages and other home costs. Several were voluntary workers, unemployed, or working part-time. A few were retired. There was no one I felt I could ask for money, so I filed the papers under the bed and tried to forget about it.

A few weeks later Jo, a friend who was working with another missions agency, called to invite me to stay with her for a weekend. The only time we could both manage was the weekend of her mission's annual meeting, so she said I could come as long as I did not mind going to that.

The appointed day arrived, and Jo met me at the station. As we walked to the meeting she asked how my job search was going. I explained my disappointments and told her about the apparently abortive idea of the mission school. She said, "You won't believe this, but the speaker tonight is Peter, one of the leaders of that mission agency!"

The original speaker for the evening had pulled out at the last minute, so they had called Peter. He should have been in China, but he'd had trouble getting a visa.

When Peter got up to speak it was as if he were speaking just to me. He told the story of his first experience with this mission. He had felt strongly called to go to Belgium for an orientation conference but had practically no money. He said to God, "I'll go, but You will have to provide the way for me to get there." He used most of his money taking the bus into Birmingham. Knowing he did not have enough money to take the train to Dover for the ferry crossing to Belgium, he nevertheless began to walk around to the train station. As he was waiting to cross the road, a friend he had not seen for years drove by, stopped, and asked where he was going.

He offered to give Peter a ride as far as London, as long as Peter did not mind going to a wedding on the way. After the wedding ceremony Peter was slipping out of the church when someone stopped him and said, "I don't know why, but I felt the Lord telling me to give you this." With that, he pressed some money into Peter's hand—just enough to take him from London to Belgium!

As I listened with growing incredulity, God tried to tell me, "If I could do it for him, I can do it for you," but I still wasn't convinced. This was one of the top leaders in this agency—of course God would provide for *him*, but I'm just little me. Things simply don't happen like that for people like me!

After the meeting Jo introduced me to Peter. He asked, "So what do you do?" "I'm trying to get a job as a teacher," I replied. "Oh yes?" he said. "Is that before or after you teach at our school?" Much to his surprise and consternation, I burst into tears, and Jo had to explain for me.

God could not have spoken any more clearly! I decided to surrender. "Okay, God," I told Him. "I will apply, and I will do what I can. But if the money is going to come in, you will have to bring it, because I can't see any way to raise it all otherwise!"

I told my parents my new plan for the next two years, filled out the application forms, and let all my family and friends know. My dad and I began to dream up creative schemes for fundraising—donor dinners, bake sales, craft sales. I took a Christmas job in a shop to help pay off my school debt. In early summer, my church let me have a table at the Village Festival to sell some of my unwanted belongings to raise money. Several people gave me one-time gifts, and offers of monthly support began to filter in.

There were no miraculous meetings, no huge, unexpected donations, but many, many small gifts, often from people I hardly knew. Before my dad and I had a chance to put any of our plans into action, I added up how much I had, how much had been promised, and what I had managed to save from my job. I discovered that slowly, quietly, and unobtrusively God had provided exactly the total I needed for my two-year commitment, including my conference fees and flight.

I always knew He *could* do it but never really believed

He *would* do it for me. Is it faith when you don't really think God will do what He says He will? Well, whatever it was, I stepped out in it! I have now been in missions for five years, and God has continued to provide for my needs, plus a few "wants" on the side! More than that, He has broadened my horizons beyond my imagination and allowed me to be part of His plan in many people's lives.

Jennie learned that raising support was actually God's business, and He has ways to bring the funds in, even through people we do not know or methods we have not considered. My husband and I experienced the same thing: people we barely knew became excited about our ministry and introduced us to people we did not know who decided to support us. People who we thought might support us didn't, while those we never expected to did. We learned that it is not up to us to convince people—God would do that. We just need to be faithful to do our part, and He is faithful to do His.

There are different methods and philosophies about raising support, from polished presentations to simply praying about needs, without talking about them, and trusting God to supply. David and Sandy, from the United States, were convinced that God had asked them to trust Him to provide for their financial needs without making them known, but their faith was tested when they needed to raise a very large amount in a very short period of time.

The summer before we left for Central Asia was one of the most hectic we have ever experienced, for obvious reasons. But on top of getting ready to move, we were also working on adopting our second child from Mongolia, a land we had lived in for six years. Along with the money the mission leadership had suggested we raise (money for flying to Central Asia, setting up a home, and so on), we also needed funds to travel to Mongolia and pay all the fees necessary to adopt our daughter. My first estimates were that we needed around $12,000 U.S. dollars to come in over the next two months, and as overwhelming as that figure was, it was what I had been praying for.

Things came to a head one day when my wife, Sandy, expressed some of her concerns regarding the financial picture. For years we had been following a principle we felt the Lord had given us—that we never solicit funds, only pray for them to come in. On this particular day Sandy wondered aloud if we should ask for help this one time since we needed so much.

Her suggestion greatly disturbed me, and I went off to pray about it. I was walking down a road, opening up my heart, and said, "Lord, I really need some encouragement regarding our finances today." A split second after I prayed the word *today,* my eyes fell upon a bunch of pennies on the ground. Now, how many times in your life have you come across a bunch of change on the ground? And how many of those times were immediately after you had prayed about a financial need?

"Lord, I think we need a little bit more than a few pennies, but if this is how you want to start to provide, thank you." I counted fifteen pennies. As I left that spot, the Lord's strategy came to me.

As soon as I got home, I gathered my wife and son together in the living room and told them what had happened and what I felt the Lord wanted us to do. First, we were not to pray for $12,000 but for $15,000 to come in over the next two months—$1,000 for each penny I had found. Second, as the Lord answered the prayers, whenever $1,000 came in, we would transfer one of these pennies from one bowl to another bowl. And we would not tell anyone we were doing this. Each of us agreed and prayed together that the Lord would show us His power.

Over the next seven or eight weeks, as we prayed daily for this need, we transferred all fifteen of those pennies, each time making a ceremony of it. In fact, even more came in. The Lord is faithful!

Besides raising support, another financial issue that holds people back from missions is debt. College students often do not realize that unpaid school loans can keep them from being accepted to serve, which can delay them from going into ministry for several years. If you want to go into missions soon after graduation, find ways to avoid building up significant debt. Pursue scholarships and grants, look into schools that cost less, or go a little slower so you can pay your way. Sometimes people will financially come alongside those who are going into ministry. Just as God can motivate people to support you in missions, He can also move them to help with tuition.

If you already have school loans to deal with, there are still options. If you are simply considering a year or two in missions, some kinds of school loans can be deferred for a time. Another option is that someone might feel led to make your loan payments for you as their way of supporting you. I heard about two Bible school students who were praying about going into missions. One student felt God leading him to stay home and work so he could support the other and pay off his loan.

As we have seen through the stories in this book, God works

with each of us as individuals, even in financial matters. Like everything else in the Christian life, seek His direction on how you should proceed, and trust Him to provide.

"Jesus, I give You my worry about my college loan debt."

"Lord, I give my financial situation to You. When my debt is gone You can have me completely, but I will give You all of me now too."

"Dear God, I offer up my lack of financial control that I may be able to give more in order to further your kingdom."

"Lord, I give You my future, my finances, my fear. Be my light and inspiration, and may you guide me in my ways to come. Take away things that distract from You, and take me further into worship with you."

"Father, I do not take Your love for granted. You are worthy. Lord, I give my life. Help me believe, help me with finances, and help me focus on You. Lord Jesus, come quickly."

"Dollars, Lord. Help me to be more giving financially to those in need. Help me to free up money for missions work as well."

"God, right now I give You my financial debt and lack of confidence in myself at times. I pray for Your help, courage, and love. Thanks"

"Who serves as a soldier at his own expense? Who plants a vineyard and does not eat of its grapes? Who tends a flock and does not drink of the milk? Do I say this merely from a human point of view? Doesn't the Law say the same thing? For it is written in the Law of Moses: 'Do not muzzle an ox while it is treading out the grain.' Is it about oxen that God is concerned? Surely he says this for us, doesn't he? Yes, this was written for us, because when the plowman plows and the thresher threshes, they ought to do so in the hope of sharing in the harvest. If we have sown spiritual seed among you, is it too much if we reap a material harvest from you? . . . Don't you know that those who work in the temple get their food from the temple, and those who serve at the altar share in what is offered on the altar? In the same way, the Lord has commanded that those who preach the gospel should receive their living from the gospel" (1 Corinthians 9:7–11, 13–14, NIV).

PART THREE:
OVERCOMING OUR WALL
OF OBSTACLES

16

Scaling the Wall

"With my God I can scale a wall."
(Psalm 18:29, NIV)

What a joy it has been to collect the stories for this book! I have been encouraged, as I hope you have, to see in actuality what I know intellectually—that God is bigger than any obstacles we may face.

We have seen that He can replace fear with peace, even in fearful situations. He can supply funds when no logical source of funds is in sight. He can orchestrate the circumstances of our lives to redirect, to guide, and to confirm what He wants us to do. He will supply our needs—whether for meaningful relationships or material things—and often surprise us by fulfilling our desires when we trust Him. He can use us, in spite of our inadequacies, if we abide in Him and allow Him to work through us.

I was impressed by several common elements in these stories. First, God speaks to His people through His Word. So many times it was during the person's private Bible-reading or during a sermon that God highlighted a passage that gave them a sense of guidance in their situation. Second, prayer—talking and listening to God—was vital to finding out what He wanted them to do. Third, God used His people, and even a few unsaved parents, to help direct those who were looking for His will. Fourth, God arranged circumstances to help guide and facilitate, from finding a pile of pennies, to colleges mistakenly refusing acceptance, to "chance" meetings with key people. I also noticed that many received guidance for long-term plans through short-term mission trips. And many found that God did not act until they stepped out in faith and obedience.

If you are considering missions, here is my advice to you: broaden and deepen your knowledge of God—through His Word, prayer, and others who know Him well. The better you know Him, the easier it is to trust and follow Him. Ask Him to direct you, and listen to Him and key people in your life. Be sensitive to circumstances that He seems to be controlling, and "push on some doors" to see if they will open. Like the missionaries who have shared their stories, you can experience what David found to be true in Psalm 18:29: *"with my God I can scale a wall."*

"Lord Jesus, I give You myself. I don't want to live a life planned by me.

I give You my thoughts—sinful and pure—and ask You to redeem them all.

I give You my fears. I give You my doubts. I give You my secrets.

I give You my hesitancy to accept fully Your love and forgiveness.

I give You my goals and my dreams; please make them line up with Your plan for my life.

I give You my imperfections; please help me to know You accept me as I am and that I don't first have to become perfect.

I give You my marriage; please may it be a picture of You and Your Church.

I give You my desires to pursue wrong actions and relationships, even when only in my fantasies.

I give You myself; please take and refine me. Please use me to bring glory to Your name.

I also give You my deepest desire of all to be intimate with You, as close as is humanly possible and even beyond, because so much is possible with You.

I give You my love, imperfect and complete.

I give You myself—Your daughter, Your coheir, Your bride."

"My fear, pride, and ignorance plague me, Lord. But Your victory in life, death, and resurrection free me from their shackles. I love You, Jesus. I thank You for forgiving my lack of trust in these areas before. But here, now and in the future, I lay them at Your feet. Open my hands. And I say, 'Here I am Lord. I have heard Your calling. Send me.'"

Acknowledgements

First, I'd like to thank all those anonymous contributors who shared their struggles and obstacles on the Wall at Urbana. Thanks for opening up your hearts for us to see and learn from. May the Lord help you scale your walls and bring you into the joy of His will for you.

To Dan Potter goes my gratitude for coming up with the creative idea of asking the students to write their obstacles on the Wall.

Thanks to Ben Bradley who spent hours sitting in front of the Wall with his laptop, taking down the comments so they could be used for this book.

I'm grateful to the many missionaries who shared their stories with me to encourage others to trust God to get them past their own obstacles. Unfortunately, I was unable to fit them all into the book, but I greatly appreciated and was encouraged by every contribution.

I want to thank all of my friends and family who faithfully prayed for and encouraged me throughout the writing process, especially Roger who took a special interest in the book.

To Michaela Dodd, my editor, thank you for your help and skill in improving the final product.

I'm also very grateful to my husband, Rick, who is a constant encouragement and support to me and whose advice I greatly value. I love you.

And, finally, thanks to our Lord Jesus Christ, who is the One who guides, provides, and overcomes every obstacle we face, enabling us to scale the wall before us and accomplish what He has given us to do. This book is really all about Him.

Cat and Dog Theology
Rethinking Our Relationship With Our Master

Bob Sjogren & Dr. Gerald Robison

There is a joke about cats and dogs that conveys their differences perfectly.

A dog says, "You pet me, you feed me, you shelter me, you love me, you must be God."
A cat says, "You pet me, you feed me, you shelter me, you love me, I must be God."

These God-given traits of cats ("You exist to serve me") and dogs ("I exist to serve you") are often similar to the theological attitudes we have in our view of God and our relationship to Him. Using the differences between cats and dogs in a light-handed manner, the authors compel us to challenge our thinking in deep and profound ways. As you are drawn toward God and the desire to reflect His glory in your life, you will worship, view missions, and pray in a whole new way. This life-changing book will give you a new perspective and vision for God as you delight in the God who delights in you.

1-884543-17-0   206 Pages

A Guide To Short-Term Missions
A Comprehensive Manual For
Planning An Effective Mission Trip

H. Leon Greene, M.D.

Drawing on his experiences from over thirty short-term mission trips, Dr. Greene gives a detailed look at the challenges and blessings faced by those who are considering such an endeavor. This one-stop guide helps make the most of this opportunity by outlining the steps to take from start to finish.

Included are great resources such as:

- Preparing a testimony
- Writing a support letter
- Getting a passport
- Forming the team
- How to stay healthy
- Immunizations needed
- Packing Checklist
- Emergency plans and disaster relief
- Useful web sites

1-884543-73-1   288 Pages

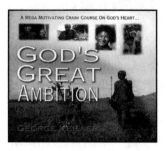

God's Great Ambition
A Mega-Motivating Crash Course On God's Heart

Dan and Dave Davidson
and George Verwer

This unique collection of quotes and Scriptures has been designed to motivate thousands of people into action in world missions. George Verwer and the Davidsons are well-known for their ministries of mission mobilization as speakers and writers.

Turn to any page and get ready to be encouraged and respond with an increase of awareness, action and ownership in sharing God's good news around His world.

1-884543-69-3   208 Pages

Operation World
Patrick Johnstone & Jason Mandryk

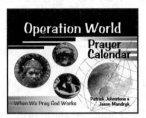

Prayer Calendar

This spiral desk calendar contains clear graphics and useful geographic, cultural, economic, and political statistics on 122 countries of the world. The *Operation World Prayer Calendar* is a great tool to help you pray intelligently for the world. Pray for each country for three days and see how God works!

1-884543-59-6   256 Pages

Wall Map
22" x 36"

This beautiful, full-color wall map is a great way to locate the countries that you are praying for each day and build a global picture. Not only an excellent resource for schools, churches, and offices, but a valuable tool for the home.

1-884543-60-X   Laminated
1-884543-61-8   Folded

For more information on how you can get involved, contact...

OPERATION MOBILIZATION — www.om.org
Operation Mobilization works in more than 80 countries, motivating and equipping people to share God's love with people all over the world. OM seeks to help plant and strengthen churches, especially in areas of the world where Christ is least known.

YWAM — www.ywam.org
Youth With A Mission is an international movement of Christians working to help make a difference in a needy world through evangelism, mercy ministry, training and education.

PIONEERS — www.pioneers.org
Pioneers mobilizes teams to glorify God among unreached peoples by initiating church-planting movements in partnership with local churches.

US CENTER FOR WORLD MISSIONS — www.uscwm.org
The USCWM produces and publishes resources to motivate and equip Christ's body to join Him in His Biblical purpose to "bless all the families of the earth" (Gen. 12:1-3). The USCWM also engages in a variety of activities toward ensuring, as soon as possible, that each distinct people group is "reached"—that a viable movement is established to evangelize and disciple each people group.

ACTION INTERNATIONAL — www.actionintl.org
ACTION is an evangelical, non-denominational missionary-sending agency that works in major urban centers of Asia, Latin America and Africa. ACTION missionaries reveal the Gospel and love of Christ to neglected and abused children and their families through practical ministries that specialize in reaching the urban poor.